Praise for *Be You, Only Better*

"Kristi Hugstad offers a balanced yet thorough, whole-person approach to self-care, equipping you with the necessary tools to maintain healthy living. If you are looking for practical steps that are easy to understand yet innovative at the same time, this book is for you. She covers exercise, diet, and healthy relationships, including prompts for self-reflection to check in so that you can experience the abundant life that you deserve. You'll be empowered with an attitude that says, 'I can do this,' so that you can 'be you, only better.' The time to thrive is now."

— **Dave Dicken**, creator of Make Someone Great Today
and crisis counselor at Crisis Text Line

"For the past thirty-five years, I have watched stress levels and resulting mental health issues increase among both the special education students I teach and the high achievers I coach. Though the two groups are different in nature, the levels of depression and anxiety in both have risen, especially in the midst of a global pandemic. I am grateful that authors such as Kristi Hugstad are tackling the issues that impact our youth, and I am especially happy to see gratitude and hope as part of her self-care regimen."

— **Jorjean Fischer**, special education teacher
and cross-country running and track coach

"As a veteran high school teacher and coach, I have witnessed students dealing with many of the issues that Kristi Hugstad addresses in *Be You, Only Better.*...I applaud her for focusing on areas such as the importance of sleep, how to maintain a healthy diet, and money and time management."

— **Dan Leer**, high school English teacher,
athletic coach, and yearbook adviser

"*Be You, Only Better* offers informed advice for young adults and parents, using science with a capital *S* to present her stories of self-help in a trusted voice. Hugstad gives easily understood examples of self-care that will resonate with readers. Chapters tell stories based on actual young adults, anchoring us in their lives and transformative behaviors (diet, managing time and money, and finding happy relationships)."

— **Dr. John Maitino**, professor at Cal Poly Pomona

"*Be You, Only Better* is an engaging book with real-life stories that quickly teach a lesson.... Each chapter is broken up into key sections, making it an easy but meaningful read. As a middle school teacher, I will encourage my students to read this book. I plan to follow these self-care approaches as well!"

— **Sara Twiss**, middle school leadership teacher

Praise for *Beneath the Surface* by Kristi Hugstad

"A must-read for anyone wanting permission to help themselves or a friend, this book reads as though it's reaching out to grab you and hold you in your time of need."

— **Regina Louise**,
author of *Somebody's Someone* and *Permission Granted*

"When you find yourself wondering what you can do, or you have a student who is struggling, here is a book that can help. It is a starting point for a conversation that just might save someone's life."

— **William Meyer**, author of *Three Breaths and Begin*

"A well-written outreach mainly to adolescents, but frankly to anyone seeking to help a family member or friend suffering with depression and suicidal ideation... A great read that's clinically relevant and helpful."

— **Nadine Levinson, DDS**,
clinical professor, psychiatry, University of California, Irvine

"My hope is that Kristi Hugstad's book *Beneath the Surface* will give teens hope and insight into their emotional lives and help them emerge stronger, as well as wiser."

— **Maureen Healy**, author of *The Emotionally Healthy Child*

"Invaluable insight and support that will help any troubled teen come through the turbulence of those years."

— **Steve Taylor, PhD**, author of *The Leap* and *The Calm Center*

"Critical to any parent, whether or not the parent realizes it... this book not only changed my life, it changed the life of my child."

— **Kevin Thaddeus Fisher-Paulson**,
columnist, *San Francisco Chronicle*

BE
YOU,
Only
Better

Also by Kristi Hugstad

Beneath the Surface: A Teen's Guide to Reaching Out
When You or Your Friend Is in Crisis

Returning to Joy:
Inspiration for Grieving the Loss of a Loved One

Returning to Joy:
Inspiration for Grieving the Loss of Your Cat

Returning to Joy:
Inspiration for Grieving the Loss of Your Dog

What I Wish I'd Known: Finding Your Way
through the Tunnel of Grief

BE
YOU,
Only
Better

Real-Life Self-Care for
Young Adults (and Everyone Else)

KRISTI HUGSTAD

Foreword by Tami Tucker, PhD

New World Library
Novato, California

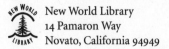

New World Library
14 Pamaron Way
Novato, California 94949

Text design by Tona Pearce Myers

Library of Congress Cataloging-in-Publication Data

Names: Hugstad, Kristi, author. | Tucker, Tami, writer of foreword.
Title: Be you, only better : real life self-care for young adults / Kristi Hugstad ; foreword by Tami Tucker, PhD.
Description: Novato, California : New World Library, [2021] | Includes bibliographical references. | Audience: Ages 14 to 18 | Audience: Grades 10-12 | Summary: "Outlines daily practices that promote physical, mental, and emotional health for young people making the transition to adulthood. The author covers practices such as journaling, exercise, healthy sleep habits, time management, and mindfulness, with brief discussions of scientific research showing the proven benefits of each practice"-- Provided by publisher.
Identifiers: LCCN 2020052363 (print) | LCCN 2020052364 (ebook) | ISBN 9781608687381 (paperback) | ISBN 9781608687398 (epub)
Subjects: LCSH: Youth--Health and hygiene--Juvenile literature. | Teenagers--Health and hygiene--Juvenile literature.
Classification: LCC RA777 .H835 2021 (print) | LCC RA777 (ebook) | DDC 613/.0433--dc23
LC record available at https://lccn.loc.gov/2020052363
LC ebook record available at https://lccn.loc.gov/2020052364

First printing, March 2021
ISBN 978-1-60868-738-1
Ebook ISBN 978-1-60868-739-8
Printed in Canada on 100% postconsumer-waste recycled paper

10   9   8   7   6   5   4   3   2   1

Contents

Foreword

*W*hy do I act the way I do? How do people change? What makes me feel the things I feel? What keeps me from going after what I truly want? Why do I feel unable to control my life and my emotions? These are the most basic questions we begin to ask ourselves early in life. They are some of the questions that clients bring to my office, but they are not unique to those struggling with mental health issues. These are basic questions that everyone should be able to answer as we navigate the challenges of life. Finding answers to these questions should not require a visit to a psychologist. Often in my practice I have lamented, *Why don't we teach more about these psychological principles, so critical to our mental health, in schools?* Children and adolescents learn about dinosaurs and rivers in distant lands, but very little about psychological health.

Kristi Hugstad learned these concepts not through structured academia but through necessity to survive a devastating loss in her own life. Through her perseverance while in pain, and through her research and salient insight, she has produced this book, a road map really, for people, young and old alike, who are struggling emotionally or who just want to be "better."

As a psychologist for almost thirty years, consulting to businesses and working in my own clinical practice, I am amazed at how well Kristi brings to life, with practical, helpful examples, some of the most critical components of what the field of psychology has to offer to those who seek greater self-understanding and self-growth, who are driven to deepen meaningful relationships, and who want to purposely set and achieve goals that will lead to living the life of their dreams. Kristi has made the complex simple and accessible, and has created, in my professional opinion, a manual that will help a great many young people.

— Tami Tucker, PhD, clinical psychologist

Preface

Today, young adults and teens are facing unprecedented times. They have the challenges of school and are dependent on parents. They struggle to establish relationships and grow more independent. Like their parents, they worry about the economy, pandemics, and global warming. They are also experiencing a world in which the prevalence of mental health issues has reached crisis levels. Young adults grapple with academic and work stress; peer, parental, and self-pressures; substance abuse; gender dysphoria; food and financial insecurities; self-harm; PTSD; anxiety and depression — and that's just to name a few. Some may worry about whether their family's business can sustain itself, and many wonder if they can afford college without accruing huge loans. Young adults may struggle with the dynamics of broken families, or they may feel pressured to decide on a career before they're prepared to plan their future. Some may be working too hard to live up to their parents' expectations or burning themselves out in sports or academics.

Even in the best circumstances, young adults deal with confusion, stress, and fear for a myriad of reasons, such as experiencing their first heartbreak from a failed romantic relationship. All of this, when not effectively managed, can lead to health problems — mental and physical.

It's difficult to be on the threshold of adulthood, to live with uncertainty, to be a novice in an adult world — especially if childhood has been hard, too. Even when childhood has seemed easy, young adults can come to feel like they're expected to build a house without understanding how a house is designed or what tools they need. My goal for this book is to give you both a plan and the tools.

Be You, Only Better was inspired by my previous book, *Beneath the Surface: A Teen's Guide to Reaching Out When You or a Friend Is in Crisis*, which provides straightforward information on the issues facing youth today. *Be You, Only Better* takes that resource a step further, outlining the day-to-day practices that promote physical, mental, and emotional health. These practices can help you become an architect of your body and mind, inspiring you to create a firm foundation and frame for the house that is your life.

Attaining physical health requires good habits that nurture the body. This may mean changing habits to cut down on sugar consumption, to get enough sleep, and to exercise more. In this book I provide the science of how your body's well-being is the catalyst for the well-being of your mental and emotional health. You are a whole, complex organism, a matrix of relationships between mind and body. Mental health also requires that you nurture healthy relationships with the people in your life and find time to practice gratitude and mindfulness.

Today, my mission is to abolish the stigma of mental illness and suicide through education and hope. As a certified grief recovery specialist, health educator, and speaker, I work with young adults who are struggling to understand themselves and the world around them. I hope *Be You, Only Better* can be a lifeline for you as you look to become who you are meant to be: a happier, healthier version of yourself.

Before I start, I want to explain why I'm so passionate about this message. I have firsthand experience with clinical depression, substance abuse, and suicide. My husband, Bill, completed suicide by running in front of a train in Dana Point, California, where we lived at the time.

Bill was depressed, and we were both in denial about how serious this was, in part because of the stigma of mental illness. This led to shame and hiding in lies. I saw the signs, and I did my best to deal with them, but ultimately, when I look back, I wish we'd had a book like this, which might have made the difference.

In the aftermath of his death, I followed the self-care steps I present in this book, and they helped me move forward. I was able to heal from the trauma of my husband's suicide and I learned to truly take care of myself, a skill that saved my life. I went on runs or swam in the ocean. I started writing what became my first book. I cut out caffeine and made sleep a priority. I cultivated positive thinking, focusing on what I was grateful for: my sisters, mother, and friends who checked in on me during my darkest times. I developed a lifestyle that went beyond healing, one that helped me move forward and thrive. I found hope in my own life. Because of this life-shattering experience and my own healing, my passion for prevention, education, and helping others emerged.

On the program for the memorial service after Bill's death, I placed an image of a monarch butterfly. That butterfly became real when one flew into the room during the ceremony.

I hope to help you transform into the best version of *you*, just like a caterpillar that transforms into a butterfly. My goal is to rid the world of stories like Bill's — and that goal starts with you.

I hope you find solace and strength in this book and in the stories of others. However, I also intend for this to be a practical guide for establishing the good habits that will contribute to your well-being. I want to give you the tools to cope and to take charge of your life by developing a lifestyle of hope and happiness. Now, more than ever before, you need tactical resources to help you maintain and improve your physical, mental, and emotional health. When you develop these habits, which soon become as natural as brushing your teeth, it's like entering a cocoon and then learning to fly. All you need is to be who you are — only better.

Introduction

I t's not the latest trend. It's not a hashtag on social media. And it's certainly not selfish. Self-care is an incredibly important part of your physical and mental health. The better you nurture yourself, the better equipped you will be to enjoy your life, reach your goals, and help and support others.

Self-care isn't just a to-do list, either. Stressing yourself out about what you *should* be doing undermines the whole point — self-care is focusing on what you *can* control by identifying your needs in real time and taking action to meet them. It's important to check in with yourself several times throughout the day and ask questions like:

- How am I feeling?
- What can I do to feel better?
- How can I help others?
- What areas in my life need nurturing?
- How can I handle my stress in the present moment?

Here's what self-care looks like in a situation most of us can relate to — a stressful, hectic morning. Let's say you oversleep and don't have time to shower before school or you'll be late. Rather than charging through the house panicked and stressed-out, snapping at anyone who might be around, you take a second to breathe. You stop and think about how you can make the day work for you — and which of your current needs are most important.

Since you know your stress will escalate and your mood will crash if you're hungry all morning, you eat breakfast. However, this doesn't leave you with enough time for a shower, so you wash up quickly and dress extra nice. These simple choices help you to not start your day stressed-out.

When you practice self-care, rather than surrender to a "bad day," you set a positive tone for the hours ahead. You take control over how you respond to the situation. The key to self-care is introspection — resisting the urge to react right away and instead taking the time to reflect and make a plan. If a plan doesn't come easily, you continue to pause and breathe, allowing your heart rate to return to normal so you can think clearly. To reduce stress, you remind yourself that the current situation is only temporary and envision a positive solution to your problem.

Of course, self-care looks different to each of us and can vary day to day — there's no one-size-fits-all formula. That said, here's one principle that helps *everyone* master self-care: making the time and effort to invest in your overall wellness, which includes the following five areas.

Five Types of Self-Care

There are five main types of self-care: physical, emotional, social, mental, and financial. Depending on your needs at any particular time, you may need to focus on one or two types more than others.

1. **Physical:** When someone mentions self-care, many think first of taking care of their physical body, and this is incredibly important for both physical and mental health. However, this doesn't necessarily mean committing to a vigorous exercise program — but if you do, that's great! The key to physical self-care is finding exertion and exercise you *enjoy* — whether that's yoga or hiking; dancing, strength training, or cycling; or best of all, a combination of several activities. In addition, good nutrition — like eating more fruits and vegetables, cutting out sugar, and drinking plenty of water — is an important component of physical self-care.

2. **Emotional:** Emotional self-care isn't about *controlling* your emotions. Good self-care means becoming more in sync with your emotions and allowing yourself to feel them. You let yourself laugh, cry, get angry — and feel exactly what you're feeling rather than ignoring or stifling your emotions. Teaching yourself to respect your emotions empowers you to have greater compassion — for yourself and others. Emotional self-care means being more mindful of the situations and thinking patterns that trigger negative emotions. Like every aspect of self-care, recognizing and respecting your emotions takes time and practice.

3. **Social:** We all need social connections and a support system of people we trust. Social self-care means

spending time with loved ones, hanging out with friends, being part of a community, and pursuing a hobby or interest with others who share your passion. Positive feelings are contagious. Since we all have different social comfort levels — some consider themselves introverts and some extroverts — social self-care looks different for everyone. But here's the bottom line: Make an effort to include happy people in your life. Happy people are contagious, and spending time with them can help you feel happier, too.

4. **Mental:** The way you think and what you think about greatly influence your sense of well-being. Mental self-care is all about keeping your mind sharp. In many ways, your brain is a muscle that requires activity and exercise to grow and develop. Mental self-care includes activities that stimulate your mind and your intellect, like reading, solving puzzles, playing chess, writing, studying, or learning a new language. Whether you're attending school or not, keep your mind constantly learning and growing.

5. **Financial:** Money isn't everything, but financial worries or problems can be a significant cause of stress and anxiety, which in turn affects your overall well-being. Financial self-care boils down to three simple steps to help you manage your finances: You increase your awareness of how you manage your money; you make a financial plan, which provides a sense of control; and you prioritize your expenses and stay on top of them. By practicing financial self-care, even if it means spending less, you avoid the stress

and anxiety that come from mismanaging money or out-of-control debt.

Nurturing yourself in these areas won't simply make you feel better, it will change your thinking and rewire your brain! That's because your brain releases different types of "feel-good" chemicals when you engage in self-care activities. By adopting healthy habits, you trigger these "happy hormones," which improve your mood and increase your happiness. This is why self-care gets easier the more you do it. It makes you happier and puts a smile on your face — and on the faces of those who love to see you happy.

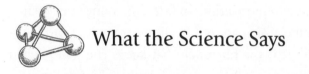 ## What the Science Says

What are these feel-good neurochemicals? They include hormones called *endorphins*, and it is scientifically proven that self-care practices increase endorphin levels in the brain. Endorphins have the same structure as morphine — a drug taken to reduce pain. Our body produces endorphins when we exercise, meditate, listen to music, eat chocolate, laugh, and have sex.

Serotonin is another hormone that regulates mood. Exercise not only increases endorphin levels but also increases serotonin levels, which is why people say that exercise can improve our mood. Recent studies have shown that exercise is so effective at this that it can be used to treat some forms of depression. Of course, don't expect pharmaceutical companies to advertise the fact that some of our best medicine is free. Another way to naturally increase serotonin levels is through sunlight — so imagine what exercising outdoors under the sun can do! ·

The precursor to serotonin is *tryptophan*, but it's harder to improve your mood by increasing tryptophan. Purified tryptophan is available as a drug in some countries, like Canada, and this has been shown to increase serotonin levels. But eating tryptophan-rich foods like milk usually doesn't, since you need to consume a whole lot of them to affect serotonin levels.

Dopamine, another so-called happy hormone, is released in response to rewarding human activity and is linked to reinforcement and motivation. In fact, dopamine is associated more with the anticipation of feeling happy than with happiness itself. It is the hormone that keeps you going when you are trying to reach a goal — whether that's finishing a marathon, getting an A on an exam, or making the football team. Increasing dopamine is pretty simple. In one scientific study using brain scans, researchers compared dopamine transmission in the brains of people listening to music they felt neutral about and to music they loved. The study found that dopamine levels increased by 90 percent when participants listened to music they loved.

Another hormone that affects our mental and emotional health is *oxytocin*. Oxytocin levels rise with physical affection like kissing, cuddling, and sex, and they also increase during childbirth, breastfeeding, and strong parent-child bonding. Oxytocin speaks to our human need for physical, social connection. Science tells us that oxytocin doesn't simply respond to pleasurable situations — it requires *physical* connections. We know this because spending time in the virtual world — while it might be pleasurable — actually decreases oxytocin levels. This hormone requires meaningful social relationships — just like we do.

How to Use This Book

Throughout this book, I periodically ask you to stop reading and pay attention to what's going on in that exact moment. These prompts for self-reflection are called "Time to Check In," and one goal is to reinforce self-reflection as a habit. However, I encourage you to stop at any time, and as often as you want, to reflect on whatever feelings and thoughts come up as you read. Self-reflection improves our quality of life and increases our longevity.

Here's how I recommend you read this book:

1. Treat reading this book as your commitment to learn new things, to adopt positive habits, and to improve yourself.
2. Remember this is *your* book (and only yours). It includes worksheets, planners, and logs for you to fill out, and I encourage you to further make it yours by marking, underlining, or noting any important ideas and sections that speak to you.
3. Don't race through it. This is not a novel. It is more like a guidebook filled with information and practices for you to explore. Sections called "What the Science Says" explain some of the research that supports the concepts, but the point isn't just to understand the information. The goal is to assimilate it

into your life as ongoing self-care. Take the reading as slowly as you need to.

4. Complete the practical assignments. Every chapter includes activities and exercises, and each ends with a "How to Get Started" section that provides simple, easy ways to begin. Effective self-care takes practice. Spend whatever time and effort it takes to master it. If you lose motivation, remember your commitment to improve yourself.

5. Have fun while reading and practicing this book! Good self-care makes us healthier and happier. Focus on making this a positive experience.

CHAPTER 1

Write It Down

When you write something down, you are able to see yourself and your life as a witness. The act of writing is itself a learning process. Sometimes emotions can feel confusing and overwhelming, and writing about those feelings can be therapeutic. So finding a time in the day to process your life is a great way to nurture your growth through self-reflection, as you can see in the story about Sophia.

When Sophia was sixteen, her parents lost custody of their five children, who all moved in with their grandmother in a ramshackle three-bedroom blue house, which had a large rubber tree plant growing in the living room. By the time Sophia was nineteen, in addition to helping with household chores, taking care of her siblings, and working at the local 7-Eleven as a cashier, she was taking two classes at a community college toward a degree in business.

Needless to say, she was busy. Sophia was also still grappling with the confusing mix of grief and relief from losing her parents. Sometimes memories kept her up at night — such as when her father was too angry to control his temper, and her mother was too high to change the baby. She felt lucky to have such a kind grandmother, who did her best to make them meals and encourage them to achieve in school.

Sophia took an English composition class at college, and her teacher was a lanky old man with a head of curly white hair. One assignment involved reading and responding to a wide range of topical issues, from whether people should be allowed to carry handguns on campus to racism to environmental issues. The professor never graded this writing; students were given credit just for doing it. Sophia enjoyed the freedom of writing without an outsider's assessment, where she could express her thoughts and feelings without judgment.

One day Sophia's teacher introduced her to *freewriting*, which is simply writing without an outline or objective. He talked about the importance of writing down your feelings and thoughts, how the act of writing is learning. As a poet, he did stream-of-consciousness writing every morning, which freed his creativity and cleared his head.

Sophia bought a sketchbook patterned with flowers and started writing in it every night before she went to bed. Her mornings were too busy for writing, since from the moment she awoke, she had many responsibilities, such as packing lunch for her younger siblings, feeding the cat, and other chores.

At first, she mostly wrote about what she had done during the day and her plans for the next day. But with time her entries went deeper. She uncovered memories of life with her parents, documented snippets of dreams, and explored feelings of loss and her hopes for the future. Sometimes, she focused solely on what she was angry about or what she was grateful for.

Through journaling, Sophia discovered a way to help process whatever was painful in her life. She found herself feeling more clearheaded, sleeping better, getting better grades, and setting goals for herself.

When her little sister wanted to play, Sophia had them write stories together about wounded cats saved by vets and what the rubber tree plant thought about the sun. They jotted ideas about why their grandmother sometimes seemed sad or how Lake Michigan seemed as big as an ocean. Through writing, Sophia discovered the size and power of her own mind.

Sophia was still busy, but somehow the time she devoted toward writing made the rest of her life feel more manageable.

The Benefits of Journaling

Do you ever feel like your days blur into one big to-do list you can't keep track of? You have to meet school deadlines, go to club meetings, work, hang out with your friends, spend time with your family, organize your desk and room, exercise, read, and so on. Have you ever felt stressed-out because, no matter how much you try, you are always behind and overwhelmed? To avoid this, here is a simple solution: journaling.

If you're busy and overwhelmed, why add one more

thing to do? Because journaling makes you more organized and efficient and can even help relieve your stress.

Most journaling experts talk about two different types of journaling: journaling to achieve professional success and journaling therapy to improve your mental health. The former would be writing down what steps you need to take to be a restaurant owner, for example, and creating a rough outline and calendar of milestones to reach in order to achieve your goals. An example of the latter would be to write down a painful memory — say, of the day your parents announced they were divorcing — as a way of untangling complex, difficult feelings.

This form of self-examination has been around a long time, and it is a powerful practice. If you want inspiration, definitely check out the many journaling blogs online, some of which are geared specifically toward high school and college students. Journaling can help anyone, regardless of age, education, interests, or writing skill.

Let's talk about how journaling can positively impact your mental health. Journaling connects you with your inner self and helps you develop good habits of self-reflection. When you journal, you are communicating only with yourself. Your journal is a safe place to be honest, to be your authentic self without worrying about being judged. This is what makes it different from posting on Instagram or talking to friends, when we often filter ourselves to avoid judgment or we present an idealized version of ourselves. Instead, journaling allows you to connect with and learn about yourself, to reflect on your strengths and weaknesses, and to consider how to improve yourself. By writing your thoughts, intentions, actions, behaviors, goals, and dreams, you get to know what makes you happy and what makes you sad. You learn who and what drain you emotionally and who and what make you happy and confident. Writing helps you examine and understand emotions when you aren't actually feeling them, so you can see them clearly.

Writing down your feelings and engaging in self-reflection is a necessary habit for good mental health. When you journal about your anger, sadness, and disappointments, you openly express and release any intense feelings and thoughts. You offload negative thoughts instead of carrying them, making your mind more peaceful. Writing about and reflecting on your emotions helps you identify stressors and feel empowered.

Journaling can also improve your self-esteem and self-confidence. Studies have shown that writing about stressful events and life traumas helps with grieving and makes us feel better not only psychologically but physically as well.

Journaling can also help you achieve goals and dreams, both personally and professionally. Keep in mind, journaling is not just reflecting on the past. It is about planning for the future. Journal about long-term goals, such as studying abroad, moving to a different city, going to graduate school, and your career. Do you want to become a doctor, writer, scientist, dancer? Write about what that means for you — more than once — and reflect on the steps you need to take to get there. Just like writing a daily to-do list, this makes your goals tangible and concrete. The simple act of writing down tasks makes you feel more organized and motivated to achieve them.

As you journal, you may see where and when you waste time and how you can manage your time better. Several studies have reported that people who write down their goals are more productive.

In addition, when you journal, even though you are just writing for yourself, you will improve your writing skills. Journaling allows you to write in a safe, no-pressure environment. Further, if one of your goals is to be a published writer or blogger, journaling can serve as a stepping-stone to larger writing projects. Since writing and speaking are connected, writing helps strengthen your verbal communication skills. Putting your thoughts down on paper (or on a screen), organizing them, and strategizing what you will say, helps you talk more concisely and clearly.

These benefits aside, when you write in your journal, you physically reduce the impact of stressors on your body. A small number of studies have shown that journaling can improve our immune system and can serve as a stress-management tool. As we all know, stress is the root cause of many human diseases.

As you can see, writing regularly can help you grow and release the potential that lies within you. Journaling can make your life both easier and happier. As you build a habit of self-reflection through journaling, it improves all aspects of your life. Mapping your future puts you on track for success. When you list your goals and write down your plans, they will seep into your actions. When you write about your past, painful emotions will be given verbal expression and released, which leads to healing. It's like talk therapy, but the person you are talking to is yourself. You bear witness to yourself and thereby learn more about yourself and about your relationship to society and the world. It is in self-reflection that we grow.

Build the Journaling Habit

Here are some tips on how to incorporate journaling into your life so that it becomes a regular habit.

Get the tools

Some people like to write in a notebook. If you are one of those people, get a brand-new notebook. It does not need to be expensive. If you want, creatively decorate the cover; add drawings or color, or stick on pictures or inspirational quotations. Some people like to journal on their tablet, phone, or computer. Experiment with pen and paper and digital journaling and see which one you enjoy more.

Commit to journaling at the same time every day

Just like developing any habit, try to journal at the same time every day. Many people journal right before they go to bed. Journaling before bedtime may help you sleep better because it clears your mind. It will also make you think about what you did during the day and how you can improve. Some people journal right after they wake up or while having their breakfast because writing energizes them for the day. However, if you miss your dedicated time, just journal at another time, and if (or when) you miss a day or two, don't be hard on yourself. Just restart.

Have fun

No matter how or how much you write, have fun with it. If journaling starts to feel like a chore, play around, switch your approach, and experiment. There is no one-size-fits-all type of journaling. Remember, just because it's a habit doesn't mean it always has to be the same. Sometimes, write only a few sentences; other times, go deep into details and analyze an event. Find the style that works best for you.

Just write

Write about anything, whatever comes into your head. Don't have any expectations, and don't edit. Remember, you are the only person who is going to read your journal. Don't try to write a certain amount. Some days you may write paragraphs and some days you may write a few sentences. Writing itself is the goal, not the amount or the stylistic quality. Pick a time, and just write.

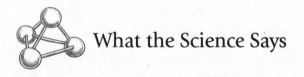 # What the Science Says

Journaling positively affects your brain

A UCLA study researched the effects on the brain of people who saw a photo of an angry or fearful face. Seeing the face increased activity in the amygdala, the brain's emotional center. However, when participants expressed their feelings in words, this decreased activity in the amygdala and increased activity in the right ventrolateral prefrontal cortex, the thinking part of the brain. This part of the brain helps us process emotions and have more measured responses. Expressing our feelings in language helps us consider them and not become impulsive or overwhelmed by them.

Journaling is beneficial to your mental health

According to the University of Rochester Medical Center, journaling can help us manage anxiety and cope with depression. By writing down feelings and concerns, we are able to track our symptoms and learn ways to find solutions. Just the act of identifying negative or destructive thoughts and feelings can help us manage them. When we track symptoms and recognize triggers, this gives us more clarity and increases potential responses. It also provides an opportunity for positive self-talk.

Journaling improves your memory

Research has shown that writing about negative emotions increases our working memory. This has implications for students with, for example, math anxiety. Intrusive and fragmented thoughts don't interfere with learning and performance if someone regularly writes and processes these emotions through expressive writing. Improving memory can also improve grades at school and performance at work.

Journaling is good for your physical health

Journaling reduces stress, which has a fundamental impact on the body. A study done on adults with various medical and anxiety symptoms found expressive writing provided clinical benefits in patients with autoimmune and inflammatory conditions, such as lupus, arthritis, asthma, and more. Researchers also found that journaling helped with blood pressure. Not only does it relieve symptoms, but it reduces stress, which in turn boosts your immune system.

Journaling helps you achieve your goals

A study by psychology professor Dr. Gail Matthews discovered that people who regularly write down their goals and dreams have a better chance of achieving them; in fact, they have a 42 percent better chance than those who do not participate in this practice. The very act of writing about what we wish for in the future makes it more likely that we will achieve our wishes.

 ## How to Get Started

Journaling prompts

Here are some journal prompts to help you dive deeper into your thoughts, intentions, actions, behaviors, goals, and dreams. Pick one whenever you need inspiration during your journaling practice.

- How are you feeling at this very moment?
- What challenges have you had today?
- What emotions did these challenges bring up?
- What did you learn from these challenges?
- What inspires you? Make a list of books, songs, activities, and more.
- What words do you need to hear? Write them down.

- Write about a friend who needed support and what compassionate things you said (or wish you'd said) to help. Then write about a time you needed support and what someone said (or what you wish someone had said) to you.
- If your body could talk, what would it say?

CHAPTER 2

Get Good Sleep

J ack was the oldest of five kids, three boys and two girls. Growing up, he often babysat his youngest sister and helped his dad with yardwork, and he studied hard for good grades. He had dreams of moving to California, but for now he was taking classes at a community college in Iowa. He longed for a girlfriend and for life near a beach, but he knew he had to work hard to achieve his dreams, so he spent most of each day doing homework and performing chores.

At night, he got into the habit of checking Instagram posts before he went to bed, and he soon found it hard to sleep at all. He would anxiously scroll through his social media late into the night, and when he did sleep, he often awoke at 3 a.m. with a feeling of dread. In the middle of the night, all his fear and anxiety would seem to crush him. To cope, he'd pick up his phone, which just fueled his anxiety.

During the day, Jack was often sleepy and couldn't concentrate. His grades slipped. In social environments, he often felt dissociated and insecure. On Instagram, one connection unfriended him, and another started dating a girl Jack had a crush on. He began to withdraw and become depressed. Because he was so tired all the time, he consumed energy drinks throughout the day — one after another.

Finally, he visited a doctor for a yearly checkup and told him about his trouble sleeping. The doctor explained to him the importance of sleep hygiene.

Per his doctor's advice, Jack began leaving his phone turned off and set it away from his bed two hours before his bedtime. He stopped eating junk food late at night, and before going to bed, he listened to music or read a book. He stopped doing homework in his bedroom and saved that space for rest and relaxation. Instead of obsessively checking Instagram, he found activities that soothed him, and he started running three times a week, always stretching before bed. When he woke up anxious in the middle of the night, he breathed deeply and slowly, counting his breaths and emptying his mind.

As Jack slept better, he felt more grounded and energetic during the day, and his grades improved. He stopped waking up in the middle of the night. His problems felt manageable. When he awoke in the morning, he felt strong and ready to start a new day.

Jack had found a cure for so much of his unhappiness, and it was something incredibly simple — something many of us take for granted.

The Importance of a Good Night's Sleep

Have you ever wished for a magic pill that could make you feel happier, get better grades, have more energy, and feel more confident? Well, there is no magic pill, but sleep just might be nature's miracle remedy — and it's especially crucial for young adults.

Clearly, getting good sleep isn't just about staying awake in history class — although it will certainly help you do that. Sleep is vital to your physical, mental, and emotional health — your overall well-being. About 91 percent of teens shortchange their sleep on a nightly basis, so let's consider for a moment what keeps people from those healing, stabilizing, empowering z's. For many young adults, the most common culprits are technology, hormones, caffeine, and overscheduled days.

As far as technology goes, have you ever found the end of the internet? Probably not, though for many people it's not for lack of trying. Today, more than ever, technology is a major contributor to sleep deprivation — particularly among teens. It's easy to stay up too late and spend too much time staring at a phone because there is always another link, another social media feed, another video, a new bit of information. It's easy to lose track of time and forget yourself, and before you know it, it's the middle of the night. While there are other negative impacts from overuse of technology, losing sleep might be the worst, since it keeps your body and mind from being able to rest and replenish.

 ## Time to Check In

Stop reading to notice and appreciate the beauty of what's happening around you at this moment.

For young adults, hormones can also affect sleep. Indeed, they are a big influence that can affect almost *everything*. During puberty, those shifting hormones aren't just impacting your emotions; they're playing around with your circadian rhythm, your body's built-in clock that signals when to sleep, wake, and eat.

According to *Neurology Live*, the shift in hormones during puberty actually makes you *want* to stay up later at night and sleep in longer in the morning. The problem? The school bell doesn't wait for you to wake up naturally. So, while you're falling asleep later, you're still getting up early, creating a sleep debt that's hard to repay.

This leads to relying on caffeine to help wake up and stay awake. Some caffeine isn't bad. Occasionally drinking a double-shot latte to get through a late-afternoon lag isn't a problem. But consuming too much caffeine during the day, every day, makes it harder to sleep at night, which leads to feeling more tired the next day, which leads people to combat that exhaustion with — you guessed it — more caffeine. That's why excessive caffeine consumption can quickly lead to a dangerous cycle of sleep deprivation.

And it's not like teens don't have things to do. Instead, from school to sports to music lessons to homework to church activities to family functions, teens tend to have too much going on, or more activities and responsibilities than they can accomplish in a day. Whether you are in school or working, your life is stressful and busy. Many young adults stay up too late not because they're irresponsible — but because they're *very* responsible!

Unfortunately, when sleep gets sacrificed, everything else suffers along with it. So here's what you can do.

Get Better Sleep

It probably seems easier said than done, but making small changes during your day can help you get more — and better — sleep. This will help you feel more rested, healthier, sharper, and more confident.

Put the phone down

Today, we're slaves to our devices, and that's not surprising. From calendars to social networking to entertainment to homework, we use our phones and mobile devices for *everything*. But if your phone never shuts off, neither will your brain — and your brain desperately needs to. Make a habit of turning off your phone an hour before bedtime. This will give your mind a chance to slow down and get ready for sleep.

Avoid caffeine during the afternoon and evening

You may enjoy the boost of a venti latte at 5:30 p.m., but that caffeine is only working against you. Artificially fueling your body when it's begging for rest only stresses it further. You might feel temporarily energized, but that energy is short-lived, and the caffeine will tamper with your body's natural desire to slow down and prepare for sleep. Try avoiding caffeine after 2 p.m., or for even better sleep, kick the habit altogether.

Get some exercise

It might seem counterintuitive, but getting your heart pumping during the day can help you feel energized (without caffeine!) *and* help you sleep better at night. The National Sleep Foundation recommends 150 minutes of cardiovascular exercise (running, walking, cycling) per week, although even ten minutes a day will help improve your quality of sleep. If cardio exercise is not your thing, weight training and yoga also improve sleep. However, do not exercise right before going to bed because it can keep you awake. Exercise no later than three hours before you plan to go to sleep.

Create a sleep routine

Like anything, sleep comes easier with practice. Create a sleep routine by following these steps:

- Wake up and go to bed at the same time each day — even on the weekends!
- Before bedtime, wind down with some light stretching, meditation, soft music, or a cup of herbal tea.
- Take deep cleansing breaths: Lie down and inhale to the count of four, hold your breath another four seconds, then exhale to the count of four.
- Make sure your bedroom is dark (no computer screen glowing in the corner), and when you wake up, open the blinds to let the light in.

This routine will signal to your brain when it's time to sleep and time to wake up. Remember, during your young-adult years, your brain — just like your body — is still growing and developing, and sleep is essential for both. Getting the sleep your mind and body need to function best is the greatest gift you can give yourself!

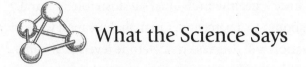 ## What the Science Says

Lack of sleep damages your brain

According to *U.S. News & World Report*, only 9 percent of American young adults get enough sleep — which should be from eight to ten hours a night, according to the Centers for Disease Control. According to recent studies, after a night without sleep, your decision-making and math-processing abilities deteriorate, and around hour eighteen (or sooner), your reaction time becomes three times slower. This is the same as being legally drunk!

After twenty-four hours without sleep, your brain forces you to have microsleeps. You don't know you are microsleeping, but you are. You miss an exit and you don't realize it, or you don't remember what happened during the last ten minutes. This is really scary. You think you are awake, but for brief moments you are not. If you stay up for more than forty-eight hours, you start hallucinating. It is theorized that your brain can only get rid of the "toxic stuff" that it accumulates during the day when you sleep. If you don't sleep, the toxic stuff just keeps accumulating in your brain and disrupts your brain function.

Lack of sleep decreases your testosterone

Lack of sleep decreases testosterone levels in both men and women. Research has shown that after just one week of sleep deprivation — or sleeping less than five hours per night — the testosterone levels of young men drop by 10 to

15 percent. Since a healthy individual's testosterone naturally declines by about 1 to 2 percent per year, that means a week of sleep deprivation will decrease testosterone levels as if someone had aged by ten years! In males, testosterone is associated with the deepening of the voice, facial hair, and increased muscle size, but it is also important for females. It is produced in the ovaries and the adrenal gland and has important effects on ovarian function, bone strength, and libido. It also plays an important role in mood and cognitive function. Decreased testosterone is associated with depression and a lack of energy.

Lack of sleep negatively impacts your immune system

Ever wonder why many students get sick during midterm or finals weeks? It's often because they are staying up late to study and are too stressed to sleep well, and sleep deprivation negatively affects the immune system. During sleep, the immune system releases proteins called cytokines, which help promote sleep and fight off infection or inflammation. A lack of sleep decreases their production. In addition, a lack of sleep has been shown to cause a decline in infection-fighting antibodies and immune cells, such as the blood cells known as natural killer cells. Research has found that just one night of poor sleep reduces the number of natural killer cells by over 70 percent. When your immune system is strong, these cells fight off viruses and bacteria. When you are sleep deprived and the cells are depleted, you're more vulnerable to getting sick.

Sleep helps you perform better on exams and at work

An interesting scientific study among college students has shown that a very effective method to increase memory and retain information is to study before going to sleep, and then get adequate rest. Here is what you do: Study material, such as for a test the next day, right before bed; go to sleep at a reasonable time (say, 10 p.m.); and then sleep for at least eight hours.

While you are sleeping, the material you have learned the night before will sink in and be retained. The next day, you will remember it better and, in theory, do better on your test. Because it increases your ability to retain information and function more sharply, sleep also makes you a better employee. Whatever your job — tracking inventory, remembering orders, collecting data — your mind will be sharper if you have a good night's sleep.

How to Get Started

The Getting-Ready-for-Bed Checklist

Complete this checklist every night to set yourself up for a good night's sleep.

- ❏ **No late caffeine:** Don't drink any caffeinated beverages after 2 p.m. At night, brew yourself a cup of herbal tea.
- ❏ **Stretch to relax:** An hour before bed, do fifteen to twenty minutes of stretching. Release stress with each stretch. Breathe deep and release.
- ❏ **Calm your body:** Cleanse your mind, body, and soul with a hot shower or relaxing bath. Wash your worries away. Add essential oils to your bathwater or steam bombs to your shower.

❑ **Put your phone down:** Thirty minutes before bed, unplug from technology. Turn off your phone. Clear your mind of outside influences.

❑ **Soothe your mind:** Right before bed, take some time to write in your journal, set your intentions, say a prayer, read, or meditate. Fill your mind with calm thoughts and welcome a night of restful sleep.

❑ **Breathe deeply:** Practice deep breathing. Inhale for four counts, hold for four counts, and exhale for four counts.

CHAPTER 3

Get Up and Move

For Chloe, exercise had never been a favorite pastime. She lived in Laramie, Wyoming, where the winters were cold and the wind often dramatic, so she preferred to stay inside. Aside from the obligatory high school gym classes, she never worked out. Her weight was considered healthy for her age, so she never felt the need for a rigorous exercise routine.

Like most girls, she thought her body had "problem areas" she wished were more toned, but instead of working toward gaining muscle mass and reducing fat, Chloe avoided pool parties and beach days and dressed in styles that flattered her body as it was. During her high school years, Chloe rarely even stepped on a scale — much less into a gym.

Now, in college, she hardly ever moved, since her schoolwork, which took up most of her time, required her to sit — either on campus or at her desk at home — for most of the day. She didn't give much thought to her diet, either. She often stayed up late gossiping over ice cream with her roommates, and her typical breakfast of sugary cereal and milk was often repeated for lunch and dinner.

Then one day during her sophomore year, Chloe went to the student health center with a bad cold. She had been feeling lethargic for months. She didn't have the energy to keep up with her tasks. She was congested and miserable, and she wasn't getting better.

The cold made Chloe realize, as much as she didn't want to admit it, that she needed to make some major changes. She was gaining weight, out of shape, and easily tired. Not knowing how else to begin, Chloe decided to take a long walk every day, regardless of the weather. Since it was April, the weather could shift suddenly from sunny and mild to windy and snowing, so she dressed accordingly. She bought a thick down coat and some comfortable stretchy leggings, and she started regularly going outdoors.

At first, her twenty-minute walks felt like they lasted forever. But after a couple of weeks, Chloe found herself walking faster and longer. She was inspired to start walking the three miles around the perimeter of her university campus, and eventually she even started to run. Depending on the day, she'd often invite a roommate or friend to join her. One of these friends, who'd been an athletic star in high school, showed her some easy toning exercises using resistance bands and inexpensive dumbbells.

Chloe couldn't believe the difference — yes, she was in better shape than ever, but she also *felt* better than ever. She was more confident and clearheaded than she'd ever been. The regular exercise motivated her to eat what her body was truly craving — whole foods like fruits, vegetables, and lean meats. For all the times Chloe had thought she couldn't possibly find time to work out, she now couldn't imagine functioning *without* exercise.

Like Chloe, pretty much everyone knows that exercise is good for us, but we can be lazy. We fall into bad habits and disregard the consequences. This is even easier when we're really busy with work or school, yet that's when we need it most, since most of our time is being spent indoors, sitting and staring at screens. Like Chloe, we can convince ourselves that we're too busy to exercise and that we're healthy enough.

Whatever excuse you find for avoiding physical exertion, the science doesn't lie: Exercise is crucial for *everyone*.

Know Your Body

Exercise isn't just about staying in shape and looking good, although those are awesome benefits! Exercise improves mental health, builds self-confidence, improves cognitive function, and boosts self-esteem and body image. And since exercise produces endorphins and promotes better sleep, it can improve mood and attitude and help reduce stress.

Today, obesity among young people is at an all-time high — and so are stress and anxiety. Rest assured, that's not coincidental! For many people, exercise becomes important only when they start to see the consequences of living a sedentary life. But developing healthy lifestyle habits when you're young provides you with a huge advantage when it comes to maintaining your ideal weight, fitness level, and overall health.

Like anything relating to health, ideal weights and fitness levels are highly individualized. What's healthy for you — and how easy or difficult it is to maintain that healthy balance — is largely impacted by your genetics. Of course, that doesn't mean you're doomed because of your genes, but it's important to consider your body type and genetic predispositions when developing an exercise routine, a diet, or any other health-focused habit. The information in this chapter is meant to help you set realistic expectations and highlight the issues that *can* be changed or reversed through lifestyle choices. As you can see from Chloe's story, improving your health isn't necessarily complicated. It doesn't require going to a gym or attending workout classes. Getting outside and walking is great for your body!

The Three Body Types

Knowing your body type can help you understand how to better manage your weight and fitness level. There are three basic body types: ectomorph, mesomorph, and endomorph. Keep in mind that many people are not entirely one type or another — you may be an "in-betweener," sharing characteristics of two types. To help you determine which type(s) you are, here is information about each one and the kinds of exercise regimes that provide optimum results.

Ectomorph

Ectomorphs have lean builds, long limbs, fast metabolisms, and delicate frames. They tend to be thin and struggle to

WHAT IS YOUR BODY TYPE?

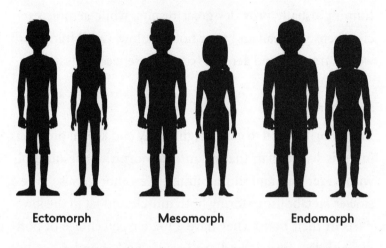

Ectomorph   Mesomorph   Endomorph

gain weight, either as body fat or as muscle. Think of an ectomorph body as looking similar to a marathon runner.

Ectomorph workout: If you're an ectomorph, focus on compound movements as opposed to isolated movements. This requires you to use more muscle groups in each exercise. Examples of compound movements include squats, which work muscles in your lower body and core; lunges with bicep curls, which work lower body and biceps simultaneously; and one-legged dips, which engage upper body, core, legs, and glutes.

Mesomorph

Mesomorphs are in between the two other body types. These bodies tend to be naturally fit and muscular. Think of mesomorphs as sprinters, who require a combination of strength, speed, and endurance to compete.

Mesomorph workout: For mesomorphs, moderate weight training usually provides great results, while aerobic exercise keeps you lean and your body fat low. Combining both weight training and aerobic (cardio) exercise is ideal.

Endomorph

Endomorphs tend to gain weight easily and keep it on. Their build is wider than that of an ectomorph or mesomorph, with wider hips and shorter limbs. Mesomorphs also have a slower metabolism, storing both muscle and fat in the lower parts of their body. They have a higher percentage of body fat with less muscle and are heavier and rounder but not necessarily obese.

Endomorph workout: Endomorphs benefit from intense aerobic exercise such as interval training. If you're an endomorph, you should focus on working your overall body. Additionally, heavy weight training with fewer reps will fire up your metabolism even hours after your workout is done.

Chloe identified herself as an in-betweener, a combination of a mesomorph and an endomorph. She learned quickly that daily walks weren't enough. She needed strength training to increase her muscle mass and raise her metabolism. Chloe was overwhelmed by the idea of adopting a new exercise routine — especially since she didn't "like" exercise! However, spending an hour a day engaged in moderate physical activity is considered crucial to your health, so she made it a priority.

Start Exercising

You don't have to go from never breaking a sweat to winning CrossFit competitions in a matter of weeks. Adopting an exercise routine doesn't have to be stressful or overwhelming — in fact, you'll be more successful if you enjoy it! You can take a dance class, go for a bike ride, practice yoga, pick up tennis, or take an online exercise class in your home. There are numerous ways to get exercise. Here are a few ways to make exercise a bigger priority in your life.

Design your fitness program

Planning to exercise will help you actually *do* it! When deciding what your exercise routine will look like, be sure to include moderate aerobic activity, strength work, and stretching. Schedule time to exercise every day just as you would schedule an appointment.

Start slowly

Start with a ten-minute warm-up and work your way up to thirty to sixty minutes of cardio. A walk gets your body loose and your blood flowing. Then increase your speed and exertion. This strategy works not just with walking but with any form of exercise — biking, swimming, using an elliptical trainer, and so on. You need to gradually increase effort, so always start at a pace that allows your muscles to get warm and loose. This also helps you avoid injury or quickly burning out. Listen to your body. Pain is your body's way of telling you something is wrong or that you may be pushing yourself too hard. If you're too sore, give yourself permission to take a day or two off.

Mix it up

Alternate activities you enjoy that emphasize different parts of your body, such as walking, swimming, dancing, strength training, yoga, and Pilates. Variety also helps you avoid getting bored with your exercise routine.

Monitor your progress

Assess your fitness program every six weeks and adjust it in order to keep improving. If you lose motivation, change things up and set new goals.

Once you've established a daily exercise plan, you'll find that it helps you in three ways — physically, mentally, and emotionally. Stick to your plan, listen to yourself and your body, and you'll find that the healthy habits you form will last your entire life!

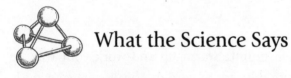 ## What the Science Says

Exercise is good for your brain

Exercise has numerous effects on the brain. It pumps oxygen and nutrients and helps release hormones, creating an environment for brain cell growth. It also promotes brain plasticity, which refers to how the brain can modify or rewire its connections and even create new neural connections. Not only does exercise rewire your brain, but it increases the size of the hippocampus, the part of the brain associated with memory, learning, and emotional regulation.

Exercise can improve your mental health

Because of these changes in your brain, exercise can reduce depression and anxiety. Many mental health conditions, especially depression, are associated with decreased neurogenesis in the hippocampus. Neurogenesis is the process of producing more neurons in the brain, and the more neurons you have, the more flexibility you have in cognition. Exercise appears to increase neurogenesis and as a result to promote cognitive flexibility. The hippocampus keeps old and new memories separate, so increased neurogenesis makes you more open to new information and less likely to be under the spell of patterns and behaviors that don't serve you anymore. In addition, exercise releases endorphins and dopamine — those feel-good neurohormones — which improve your body's ability to respond to stress by increasing communication between the central and sympathetic nervous system. Regular aerobic exercise has also been shown to increase the size of the hippocampus, promoting enhanced memory and learning.

Exercise improves your physical health

There are so many positive physical effects of exercise on the body that to discuss all of them would take an entire book! Here is a short list of advantages: It controls weight and prevents obesity; it helps manage blood sugar and insulin levels, which cuts the risk for type-2 diabetes; it strengthens bones and muscles; and it reduces the risks of some cancers, like colon, breast, uterine, and lung cancer. Exercise is also good for your heart and reduces the risk of cardiovascular disease.

Exercise helps you sleep

Exercise improves sleep by increasing your body temperature, which gives you a feeling of calm and relaxation. It can also regulate your circadian rhythm, which is your body's inner clock controlling alertness or sleepiness. However, don't exercise right before going to sleep. Exercise earlier in the day, so you can relax and slow your heartbeat after a workout.

Exercise improves your self-esteem

Exercising may seem hard at first, but once you get started, it becomes easier because exercise increases the sensitivity of dopamine receptors, which signal reward. Those rewards feel good and improve your self-esteem. Exercise can make you feel more positive and confident, increasing self-acceptance and improving your overall view of yourself. Exercise helps you be the best you can be, in part because exercise fosters the feeling that you *are being* the best you can be!

How to Get Started

Track your movements!

It's easy to get lost in a to-do list and not move your body. So put moving your body on every list, and keep track of what you do in a "movement log" like the one below (make blank copies from this book, or download and print it from my website: https://www.thegriefgirl.com/be-you--only-better.html).

For at least thirty minutes each day, walk around the neighborhood, go for a hike, jog on the beach, do yoga at home, or attend exercise classes online or in person.

MOVEMENT LOG

Week of (date): _____	Activity (if more than one, list all)	Duration
Monday		
Tuesday		
Wednesday		
Thursday		
Friday		
Saturday		
Sunday		

CHAPTER 4

Embrace Nature

Diego lived in Denver with his father, who worked for a landscaping company. Meanwhile, Diego worked in an accounting office, and every day seemed the same as the one before.

All day long he sat in a gray-walled cubicle plugging data into a computer and looking at numbers on a screen. During the week, he spent his evenings on a couch watching YouTube videos. On the weekends he usually met his girlfriend, Clara, at bars, and they sometimes danced.

Diego spent 95 percent of his time indoors. He often didn't even know what the weather was. At night he was exhausted, but he never felt like he slept well, and he often had a hard time waking up in the morning. A gnawing, unfocused anxiety settled in his gut.

While Diego felt drained and tired all the time, his colleague Max seemed to burst with energy. One day, while eating in the lunchroom, the only one with windows, Max invited Diego to join him for one of his weekend adventures, which involved hiking and climbing. They made a plan for that Saturday.

Diego and Max drove to Boulder and hiked the Mesa Trail. Diego was astonished by the different shades of green, the wildflowers, the smell of pine. They saw chipmunks and magpies, which Max told him were smart like crows. When Diego returned home, he researched the various flowers he'd taken pictures of: columbine, wallflower, Indian paintbrush.

That night Diego felt a different kind of exhaustion; he felt peaceful. He slept deeply and dreamed about crossing a river where a deer waited on the other side.

Afterward, on weekends he often took Clara for walks instead of to bars. They sometimes hiked on the plains and experienced a different kind of nature. They saw hawks soaring in the sky, blackbirds perched on cattails in ponds, spiky yucca plants blooming with thick white flowers, and prairie bindweed littering the ground with white and pink petals. When he showed pictures of bindweed to his father, he laughed and said, "That's what I'm pulling out of gardens every day!"

As Diego discovered the beauty of nature, his weeks felt less tedious. Whenever he could, he walked in his local park, where he could smell the fresh grass and watch the magpies and robins. He looked forward to his weekend hikes and became stronger, healthier, and even lost a little excess weight. When he talked with his extended family in Mexico, he promised that when they visited, he would show them the magic of nature where he lived.

Nature is a powerful force. It shapes the earth, and it nourishes and sustains all life. But you know what? Nature also makes *you* powerful. You feel at one with something bigger than yourself.

Whether we are hiking in the mountains, watching the waves gather and crash onto a beach, listening to a flock of birds sing at a park, or watering and caring for a garden, the experience of nature broadens our horizons and increases well-being. Even in cities, plants and animals surround us in parks and small gardens, which can be planted on balconies or near a window.

We are not meant to be indoors all the time and especially not in front of a screen. Like all living things, our bodies were created out of the mysterious force of nature, and getting in touch with that source can transform your life.

Go Outside

Of course, for most of us, school, work, studying, and sleeping usually require us to be inside, but we *can* carve out some time each day to enjoy the outdoors — and it doesn't have to be hours. In fact, scientists have found that spending two hours a week in nature promotes good health and well-being. That's less than twenty minutes per day. Here's advice for how to do it.

Exercise outdoors

Working out outside is the perfect way to get both exercise and fresh air. To experience nature, go for a run in a favorite park or take a hike in some nearby hills. Even a ten-minute walk in the morning and another in the evening can help you get both your nature and cardio fix. On your walks, pay attention to nature itself, such as the wildlife you meet and how the trees change with the seasons.

Get animals in your life

There are countless reasons animals can improve your overall well-being. For example, being a dog owner is particularly beneficial because it forces you to get outside! From daily walks to bathroom breaks to trips to the dog park, your furry friend will make sure you get your nature fix. However, any kind of pet provides companionship, such as a cat or even lower-maintenance pets like birds and fish. If you can't get a pet, there are other options! Bird and hummingbird feeders bring the beauty of the avian world close to you. You can offer to pet-sit for a friend or walk their dog. You can visit parks to enjoy trees and wildlife, even if that's mainly squirrels and chipmunks, and you can volunteer at an animal shelter. Just giving the living world around you more attention can enhance your life.

Develop an outdoor hobby

Any goal is easier to attain when you really enjoy what you're *doing*. Spending more time outdoors is the perfect excuse to pursue a fun hobby or activity that puts you out in the sunshine. If you want to be more active, try hiking, or if you prefer something more relaxing, try gardening, picnicking in a park with friends, or simply meditating in nature. Some neighborhoods have community gardens or opportunities to volunteer with groups that plant trees or other native plants.

Try biking, skateboarding, boating, or skiing. Or, as you develop a regular journaling practice, do your writing outside!

Mix up the everyday

When it comes to spending more time outside, it helps to get creative. Don't think so much about *adding* activities to your already busy schedule; just replace the setting! Encourage your family to eat meals al fresco during warmer or sunnier days. Suggest your study group meet at the park rather than the library. Invite colleagues or friends to join you for a hike, a bike ride, or a favorite outdoor hobby. Take the time to be social — outside!

The world can feel pretty overwhelming at times — for everyone. But spending time outside will remind you how amazing this world really is — and what a wonderful part of it you are.

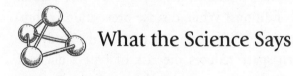 ## What the Science Says

Nature changes your brain

According to Harvard Health, a walk in nature decreases activity in the prefrontal cortex, which is active when the mind is focused on negative thoughts and negative emotions. In addition, nature can increase oxytocin, the hormone that fosters nurturing feelings; dopamine, which fosters a sense of reward and well-being; and another important chemical, serotonin. Just twenty minutes three times a week can make a difference!

Nature reduces anxiety, stress, and depression

Talk about a cure-all. If you're feeling stressed, overwhelmed, down, anxious, sluggish, or depressed, the great outdoors can be an effective treatment. According to the American Heart Association, your brain can benefit from a "journey back to nature." That could be due to the fact that human beings are wired to be outside; we evolved in nature, after all.

There's a reason a forest view helps hospital patients who are feeling down — nature is just good for the soul.

But beware: Not all outdoor settings have the same effect. Another study found that a ninety-minute walk in nature decreased worry and stewing on negative thoughts, but the same walk in an urban setting did not have the same benefits.

Nature can help prevent disease

That same walk in nature also helps prevent some chronic illnesses and conditions! While disease prevention is complex, according to one University of East Anglia study, exposure to green space reduces the risk of type-2 diabetes, cardiovascular disease, premature death, preterm birth, stress, and high blood pressure.

Nature can improve focus

With so much stimulation constantly bombarding us, it's no wonder people report feeling greater mental fatigue. We all need to take breaks from our screens, work, social media, and endless to-do lists. Spending time in a natural setting combats that fatigue, restoring the brain's ability to focus and sharpening problem-solving skills.

Nature makes you kinder

There's something about nature that provides a sense of perspective, and that perspective helps us behave in a calmer and more thoughtful manner. Marveling at the beauty in the world isn't just enjoyable — it can actually make you a better person. A study published in the *Journal of Environmental Psychology* identified a connection between people's tendency to perceive natural beauty and prosociality, that is, being kind and generous. And get this: The more beautiful the scenery, the more helpful the person who experiences it becomes.

Nature improves your self-esteem

A very interesting study showed that even one wilderness expedition increased self-esteem and connectedness in 130 adolescents. Another study of a ten-week Wilderness Adventure Therapy intervention in Australia also showed that participants displayed improved self-esteem as well as task leadership skills. When your self-esteem improves, your confidence to lead and to make decisions improves.

How to Get Started

Explore your senses

While outside, observe your sensations. Acknowledge what you see, smell, feel, hear, and even taste. Tap into the physical world and your very being.

Begin by inviting mindfulness: As you sit in nature,

take three deep cleansing breaths. Let your thoughts go and breathe in the bounty of nature. For as long as you can, simply be present to whatever you notice. Then pick up your journal and describe your sensations.

- What do you see? What colors and light? What objects?
- What do you hear? What sounds are made by wind, leaves, and animals?
- What do you smell? What do the smells remind you of?
- What sensations do you feel? Rub the ground or hold a rock. How does the breeze feel on your skin?
- What do you taste? Breathe through your mouth or chew a stalk of grass.

CHAPTER 5

Cut Down on Sugar

Alexis was a high school student who lived in a suburb outside of Athens, Georgia, with her parents and her dog, Dexter. When she wasn't at school or studying, she babysat to earn money for clothes, food, and entertainment.

She spent most of her money on food, specifically on her favorite candy and cola from the gas station across the street from her school. She loved to pour sweet-sour powder on her tongue, followed by a sweet, bubbly drink.

To keep up with her busy schedule, and because she felt tired all the time, Alexis used sweet snacks and drinks to help perk up her energy. She blamed her tiredness on the heat and the humidity, and drinking a cola between classes was easier and faster than trying to eat a whole sandwich.

Over time, Alexis started experiencing extreme highs and lows, and when she slumped, the sugar and cola didn't help as much as they did before. So she consumed more, sometimes drinking five cans of cola in a day. She became irritable, and one day when her parents asked her to walk Dexter, she screamed, slammed her door, and cried.

Another day, in her AP physics class, she couldn't concentrate on what the teacher was saying. She looked out the window at the track field and felt her hands shaking. She laid her head over her arms on the table, and when she raised her head again, she realized she had tuned out the last ten minutes.

In the evenings, Alexis never had an appetite for dinner. After eating small bites, she would sneak candy into her room and eat a whole package. However, she had trouble sleeping, and she often woke up with a heavy head and a dry mouth.

Alexis also began gaining weight, mostly around her gut, and she developed acne. One year, she developed six cavities. She felt more and more like her body was sinking, and she became depressed. She developed social anxiety because of her acne and weight, and she stopped seeing her friends as much.

Her parents became concerned and suggested she see a nutritionist. She resisted but eventually went. The doctor asked her to write everything she ate or drank that day — sweet cereal, four colas, a supersize bag of Skittles, a bar of chocolate, and a hamburger. After seeing the list, the doctor told her if she didn't cut down on sugar, she could develop diabetes.

Alexis decided to change her bad food habits. She started eating dinners with her family and drinking sugar-free electrolyte drinks. At first the sugar cravings were hard, so she chewed gum. But it worked. She began sleeping better, had more focus at school, and had more energy. Not the hyper, shaky energy from before, but a calm, steady energy, like being plugged into an electrical outlet rather than exploding like fireworks and then burning out. Her acne began to clear. She became more social. To satisfy her sour-sweet cravings, she ate raspberries or squeezed lemon in soda water. Plus, with the money she saved, she bought a new dress for the prom.

Alexis's eating habits might sound extreme, but they aren't unusual. In fact, this country's sugar obsession is as American as, well, apple pie — which also happens to be made of sugar. The average American consumes seventeen teaspoons (sixty-eight grams) of sugar a day, and half of that comes from beverages like sodas and sweetened coffees.

It's a familiar temptation: It's two o'clock, and you're starving. Dinner isn't for hours and lunch was an eternity ago. You've got ten minutes between classes, so you grab a candy bar from the vending machine and scarf it down so fast you almost inhale the wrapper.

For many of us, sugar — in its countless forms — is a go-to fix for practically *every* situation. Grab-and-go snacks are often processed and sugar laden. Celebrations require ceremonial treats (cake, anyone?). A bad day can always be combated with a pint of mint chocolate chip ice cream. But if you're eating too much sugar, you should know how those sweet treats are impacting your health.

Eat Healthier

Shunning sweets is certainly a task easier said than done — especially during the young-adult years. Processed foods are often cheaper, more convenient, and readily available. Cutting sugar out of your diet might feel overwhelming, but don't stress; being healthier doesn't mean never having another bite of birthday cake or shunning dessert forever. Make positive choices every day, and this will leave you happier and healthier than before — with or without a cherry on top.

Lowering your sugar intake may be simpler than you think. Try making a few of the following changes.

Read the labels

Becoming more thoughtful about your diet is a process. Start by reading the nutritional labels on the food you buy. These list the amount of fat, carbohydrates, and protein per serving. Sugar is listed under carbohydrates, and it is further broken down into "added sugars." This refers to the sugars that were added to the food during manufacturing, as opposed to the naturally occurring sugars in other ingredients.

For example, an apple may contain fifteen grams of sugar, but the same apple made into applesauce could have thirty grams of sugar — fifteen grams naturally found in the apple, and fifteen more as "added sugar" to make the sauce even sweeter. Avoid added sugars whenever possible. In 2016, the FDA published new requirements for the Nutrition Facts label for packaged foods. The main goal of these requirements is to reflect new scientific information on the link between diet and chronic diseases such as obesity. As shown in the example, one of the new requirements for food labels is to include "added sugars,"

Nutrition Facts

4 servings per container
Serving size 1 1/2 cup (208g)

Amount per serving
Calories 240

	% Daily Value*
Total Fat 4g	**5%**
Saturated Fat 1.5g	**8%**
Trans Fat 0g	
Cholesterol 5mg	**2%**
Sodium 430mg	**19%**
Total Carbohydrate 46g	**17%**
Dietary Fiber 7g	**25%**
Total Sugars 4g	
Includes 2g Added Sugars	**4%**
Protein 11g	
Vitamin D 2mcg	10%
Calcium 260mg	20%
Iron 6mg	35%
Potassium 240mg	6%

* The % Daily Value (DV) tells you how much a nutrient in a serving of food contributes to a daily diet. 2,000 calories a day is used for general nutrition advice.

in grams and as a percentage of the "daily value," or the daily recommended amount.

Don't drink sugar

Americans *drink* nearly half their sugar intake, so for many people, the most effective way to reduce their sugar consumption is to cut out the sugary drinks. As a rule, avoid beverages with added sugar — like sodas, sweetened coffees and teas, fruit juices, and sweet cocktails. If you like sugar in your tea and coffee, try a healthier alternative sweetener like stevia or a splash of cream. Also, fruit juices have a lot of fructose, so only indulge in them once in a while, and read the label to make sure they're 100% juice. Most of all, when you're thirsty, drink good, old-fashioned water.

Maybe you already know this. It's a simple equation: water = good, soda = bad. But to inspire you (or maybe scare you), on the next page I've shared an infographic developed by Niraj Naik from the Renegade Pharmacist that summarizes what happens within one hour of drinking a can of Coke (but it applies to all colas).

A can of cola contains the equivalent of ten teaspoons (thirty-nine grams) of sugar, which immediately causes very high levels of glucose — blood sugar. The reason that you don't vomit after consuming that much sugar is because of the cola's carbonation and phosphoric acid. To get rid of this high level of glucose, multiple organs in your body start to process it, such as your pancreas and kidneys. Since a single can equals 100 percent of your daily carbohydrate allowance, that sugar will be converted to fat, along with the carbohydrates in the burger or pizza you probably ate with it. Partly inspired by the soda's 32 milligrams of caffeine, your kidneys

WHAT HAPPENS ONE HOUR AFTER DRINKING A CAN OF COLA

1   **FIRST 10 MINUTES**

10 teaspoons (39 grams) of sugar hit your system (100% of your recommended daily intake). You don't immediately vomit from the overwhelming sweetness because phosphoric acid cuts the flavor, allowing you to keep it down.

2   **20 MINUTES**

Your blood sugar spikes, causing an insulin burst. Your liver responds to this by turning any sugar it can get its hands on into fat. (There's plenty of that at this particular moment.)

3   **40 MINUTES**

Caffeine absorption is complete. Your pupils dilate, your blood pressure rises. As a response your liver dumps more sugar into your bloodstream. The adenosine receptors in your brain are now blocked, preventing drowsiness.

4   **45 MINUTES**

Your body ups your dopamine production, stimulating the pleasure centers of your brain. This is physically the same way heroin works, by the way.

5   **60 MINUTES**

The phosphoric acid binds calcium, magnesium, and zinc in your lower intestine, providing a further boost in metabolism. This is compounded by high doses of sugar and artificial sweeteners, also increasing the urinary excretion of calcium.

6   **>60 MINUTES**

The caffeine's diuretic properties come into play (it makes you have to pee). It is now assured that you'll evacuate the bonded calcium, magnesium, and zinc that was headed to your bones, as well as sodium, electrolyte, and water.

7   **>60 MINUTES**

As the rave inside you dies down, you'll start to have a sugar crash. You may become irritable and/or sluggish. You've also now, literally, pissed away all the water that was in the cola, but not before infusing it with valuable nutrients your body could have used for things like even having the ability to hydrate your system or build strong bones and teeth.

Adapted from the Renegade Pharmacist, https://therenegadepharmacist.com/what-happens-one-hour-after-drinking-a-can-of-coke/. Content based on article by Wade Meredith.

will cause you to urinate more, which will actually make you dehydrated. Which is ironic, since you drank the cola to quench your thirst. Then, after one hour, you experience a sugar crash and become irritable and sluggish — and long for another soda to perk you up again. This is how cola becomes addictive.

Now, if you replace the cola with your favorite energy drink, you multiply the harmful effects by two or three times. No, I'm not kidding. Most energy drinks contain 100 to 200 milligrams of caffeine (and other stimulants) in each can. Instead of these drinks, have a can of flavored carbonated water, or soda water with a slice of lemon or a splash of juice.

 ## Time to Check In

When was the last time you ate and drank? In good or bad ways, how might this be affecting how you feel right now?

 ## What the Science Says

Sugar negatively affects the brain

If you've ever eaten too much sugar, you know how awful it can make you feel. From headaches to stomachaches to dizziness and nausea, a sugar overload can be hard on the body. What you might not realize, however, is that sugar also negatively impacts your brain — and that impact is worse for young adults than any other age group. In fact, excessive consumption of sugar damages areas of the brain, like the hippocampus, responsible for learning and retaining information.

Sugar can cause depression

It's easy to drown your sorrows in a pint of ice cream at night or eat your stress away with a bag of gummy bears. However, these coping tactics aren't just unhealthy — they actually amplify feelings of anxiety and depression. That's because, according to Healthline, eating too much sugar causes your body to release insulin, the hormone responsible for stabilizing sugar levels within the blood. When you binge on the sweet stuff, those sugar levels spike, causing insulin to come surging in. Those dramatic shifts in blood glucose levels leave you feeling anxious, more depressed, and totally drained.

Science has even shown that sugar can both lead to and exacerbate depression. A 2017 study showed that men who ate sixty-seven or more grams of sugar each day were 23 percent more likely to be diagnosed with depression within five years.

Too much sugar damages your whole body

For one, sugar causes excess bacteria in your mouth, which can lead to cavities. Almost everyone knows that. However, did you know it also damages your skin, liver, pancreas, kidneys, and arteries? The negative effect on the skin is due to harmful molecules called AGEs, or advanced glycation end products, which age your skin. Sugar has also been linked to acne. As for the liver, sugar in the form of fructose or high-fructose corn syrup causes inflammation and fatty buildup, which in turn can lead to liver disease. In addition, the inflammation from excess sugar can affect the arteries, and thereby stresses the heart.

Sugar is harmfully addictive

Overconsumption of sugar causes addiction through its chemical process on the brain. When sugar is consumed, the brain releases excess dopamine, followed by a crash that then requires another fix, creating a vicious cycle, similar to that of drugs or alcohol. The release of dopamine alters the brain's reward system: You experience a temporary high, and when you crash, you need another fix. This in turn can lead to the behaviors of bingeing, withdrawing, and craving, leading to a pattern of self-medication that may result in obesity or an eating disorder.

How to Get Started

Track your sugar

In order to be more aware of how much sugar you are consuming, for one week, use the log on pages 61–62 to keep track of your sugar intake every day. You can make blank copies from this book, or download and print it from my website: https://www.thegriefgirl.com/be-you--only-better.html.

Write down your main sugary choices each day. These choices include fruit juices, energy bars, soda, and whatever other sweet foods you eat. Be sure to include all drinks containing sugar (as well as sugar added to coffee or tea). Read the label or google the item to find out how many grams of sugar it contains, and write it in the appropriate column. Tally up your total intake for each day.

Men should not have more than thirty-six grams of sugar a day, and women no more than twenty-five grams. If your daily totals are higher than these amounts, look back at your list and identify foods and drinks that you could easily eliminate and what healthier alternatives you might substitute in their place. If your consumption was too high only on certain days, try to remember what was going on those days that led you to overindulge. For example, if your Tuesdays are super busy and you eat candy from a vending machine on the fly, strategize how you might avoid doing that next Tuesday. Or if your boss puts out doughnuts on Fridays and you ate two this week, make a plan to eat a healthy breakfast before work so you won't be as tempted next week. Set yourself up for success.

SUGAR LOG

Week of (date): _____	Sugary foods and drinks consumed	Grams of sugar
Monday		
Monday total sugar intake		
Tuesday		
Tuesday total sugar intake		
Wednesday		
Wednesday total sugar intake		
Thursday		
Thursday total sugar intake		

SUGAR LOG *continued*

Week of (date): _____	Sugary foods and drinks consumed	Grams of sugar
Friday		
	Friday total sugar intake	
Saturday		
	Saturday total sugar intake	
Sunday		
	Sunday total sugar intake	

CHAPTER 6

Manage Your Time

From the outside, Max looked like the quintessential "well-rounded" kid. He lived in the suburbs of Omaha, Nebraska, where he was an excellent student and was active in sports, extracurricular activities, and his church youth group. On top of that, he had many friends and a full social life. As he started his senior year of high school, he stacked his schedule with a full academic load, played on the soccer team, took piano lessons, and since he was getting ready for graduation and college, he got a new part-time job at a local clothing store.

Of course, Max also wanted to enjoy every minute of his final year of high school, which included spending as much time as possible with his girlfriend, friends, and family. Since Max had always kept himself busy and handled his responsibilities dependably, he wasn't worried about adding a job into the picture.

But less than a month into the school year, Max started feeling overwhelmed. He was frequently late to soccer practice, forgot to turn in two homework assignments, and repeatedly canceled plans with friends when he realized at the last minute that he'd forgotten an assignment or another commitment.

One October day he was driving home from soccer practice. The maple leaves were turning red, the sun was shining, but Max was exhausted and anxious. He'd had a dream the night before in which he realized he had not made it to an important class; he tried to find it, but he got lost in the school. As he was driving, he thought of all his homework, his piano recital, and the upcoming game. He panicked. He took a wrong turn and ended up at the local gas station, but he didn't need gas. When he came home, he went into his room and took a deep breath. He was scattered and unfocused, and he realized he needed to do something.

While Max had always considered himself organized, he felt anything *but*. He decided he had two options: simplify his life by quitting either his job, sports, or extracurricular activities, or learn to manage his time better. He hated the stress he felt as he tried to fit everything in, but he genuinely loved every aspect of his life, so he decided he had to teach himself to prioritize essential activities and get a handle on his schedule from day to day.

Using a time-management app on his phone, Max filled his schedule with his most important responsibilities first. He designated time each day for homework and studying during the hours he wasn't working. He added his work schedule, padding it with travel time so he wasn't stressed about being late or feeling pressure to leave early. With these "nonnegotiable" activities in his schedule, Max had a better sense of what he could and couldn't commit to. He worked with his piano teacher to find a regular time that worked better for his schedule.

With a schedule set, Max could make commitments and stick to them. If he had a big math test coming up in a few days, he'd turn down invitations from friends. Prioritizing schoolwork before his social life wasn't fun, but neither was hanging out with friends when he was stressed-out about incomplete homework or an upcoming test.

This way, spending time with his girlfriend and friends was relaxing — in fact, it felt like a reward. Today, with his time managed effectively, Max is rarely overwhelmed or stressed-out. His schoolwork and work schedule are priorities — but he also fills his calendar with *anything* that's important to him, including hobbies and social events. That way, he can enjoy them without stressing out about what he's *not* doing, and he can enjoy the shift of seasons and the moment without worrying about all he needs to do.

Time Management Means Managing Priorities

Max's time-management skills may seem pretty conventional, but for him they were very effective. That said, everyone is different, and Max's hyperorganization may not be your cup of tea.

For example, some people find typing everything in a master planner or scheduling app to be too overwhelming. They find it easier to simply jot tasks down in a notebook and stick it in a backpack or purse. If you have a good memory, you may decide not to write down some things at all.

What's important to remember is that time management isn't about cramming everything possible into your schedule — there are still only twenty-four hours in a day. Time management is about prioritizing what's most important to you and creating a schedule that allows you to fulfill your responsibilities and reach your goals without feeling stressed-out or overwhelmed.

Time management isn't a single skill. Effectively managing your time requires a variety of skills tailored to your life and brain. Some of these important skills include organization, prioritization, and planning. If you are organized in every aspect of your life, your chances of success are far better. From an organized calendar to an organized bedroom to an organized computer, this skill helps you spend less time looking for things or feeling overwhelmed by chaos, and more time getting things done. This means you need to prioritize your activities. Finally, creating a clear plan on how you'll accomplish every responsibility or attend every activity will help you follow through.

 ## Time to Check In

Take three minutes right now to sit with your breath. Breathe deep and reset. Then return to your reading, and your day, refreshed.

Let's talk about Max again. Max has a very organized computer. He has folders for each activity, and some folders — like for school — have subfolders for each class he is taking. He saves his files in the appropriate folder using clear, logical names so he can find them easily.

He also has a system to prioritize tasks. For example, when he has a big test, that's an "A" priority — and to remember that, he types a big, bold A next to it on his schedule. Family dinners are also a big priority for Max — as is, of course, his family — so he tries to finish his responsibilities by 7 p.m. most nights of the week.

Max is a planner by nature. He plans his week every Sunday evening, and then every night before he goes to bed, he checks his planning app so he can feel on top of the day ahead.

Max plans because it helps him feel less stressed and able to accomplish more. That's the beauty of effective time management — it makes you more likely to be and feel successful and allows you to enjoy hobbies and activities you love without neglecting other responsibilities.

Practice Time Management

Here are a few planning tools to get you started living a less-stressful life — no matter how busy you are. Cultivating your organizational skills will help you feel more confident and can improve your performance, productivity, and effectiveness. Once you get the hang of time management, it creates a buffer against stress and helps you to lead a satisfying, balanced life. Like any life skill, good time management isn't instinctive or innate. Practice and repetition are the keys to success!

Find out how you're spending your time

Before planning, it helps to assess how you normally spend your time. With that in mind, for one week, use the daily planner (page 74) to track everything you do in a day, filling it out with all your activities and the time they take. Once you have a clear view of your everyday activities, you'll be able to better prioritize your tasks and recognize where you may be wasting time. Also, write down everything — even sleep! You won't necessarily need to schedule sleeping, bathing, and eating, but it's good to know how much time they take. These are the essentials you need to work around as you schedule everything else.

Choose a method and budget your time

Consider what would be the best, most convenient way for you to plan and keep track of your schedule. This could be a calendar, a section of your journal, a website, an app, a notebook, or the monthly and daily planners in this chapter (pages 73 and 74). You may try several methods before you choose one that works for you. Then fill them out and budget your time. How long do you expect each activity to take? Add another 25 percent as a buffer against unanticipated disruptions.

Say no when you need to

Say no to things you don't want to do, don't have time to do, or don't want to commit to doing. Once you make a decision, stand your ground. Learning to say no is a skill you'll use for a lifetime. Don't overschedule yourself so that you can't be fully present in the things you do. If you don't want to say no, you need to schedule the activity to give yourself the time you need.

Do the worst thing first

What is the thing you are avoiding the most? Do not procrastinate what needs to be done — sometimes the best thing to do is to tackle what you've been avoiding first. Prioritize your time, and evaluate what needs to be done based on importance.

Think small and embrace mistakes

Set small goals that you can easily achieve. Messy room? Organize your desk. Have a big exam coming up that requires hours of reading and study? Schedule one-hour study blocks over several days, and take ten-minute breaks in between, or schedule a notes review every day for a week so you won't have to cram at the last minute.

Also, remember that nobody manages their time perfectly. Mistakes mean you took action, which means you gained experience, and you'll learn from the inevitable slipups.

Prep the night before

Do you sometimes find yourself frantically getting organized in the morning before heading out the door? Instead, each night before bed, go over the things you need for the next day. Visualize your day and take mental inventory. Do you have clean clothes to wear? Is the forecast predicting rain? Do you have lunch packed? Is your alarm set? With these details ironed out, your departure the next day will be much more relaxed.

Make sleep a priority

This is one area where many people shortchange themselves. Research shows that students who achieve mostly As and Bs in school average more sleep than those who receive Cs, Ds, and Fs. At times, you may have had to stay up late to finish an assignment because you misjudged how much time it would take. To avoid that happening in the future, estimate how much time you think it will take, and tack on another 25 percent.

Sleep deprivation also compromises the immune system, which can lead to getting sick. Spending time sick at home will cause additional stress. Prevent this by budgeting nine hours of sleep in your daily schedule!

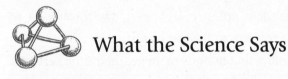 ## What the Science Says

Time management makes your brain function more efficiently

Time management is a way to avoid multitasking because you are devoting chunks of time to each activity or task. The University of London found that multitasking is inefficient. It even lowers your IQ! When you work on a single task, you use both sides of your prefrontal cortex, while if you multitask, each side is forced to work independently, which causes you to forget details and make more mistakes.

Time management can reduce anxiety

In a study of nursing students, students who were given time-management education and used the new skills reported experiencing less anxiety. If you organize your time, you are less likely to feel overwhelmed and more likely to feel in control.

Time management can improve your performance

A study of engineering students at Baylor University concluded that if they incorporated time-management study skills in a course, the retention rate of the material increased from 67 to 83 percent. The average GPA increased from 2.59 to 3.13. This study suggests that through learning the skill of time management, you can perform better.

Time management can increase work and life satisfaction

A study revealed that students who perceived that they had control of their time reported more positive evaluations on their own performance in their work and their life. They also had a reduction in stress and a clearer sense of their roles and responsibilities. This element of control over their time increased their well-being.

 # How to Get Started

Manage your time

You have a lot of things to keep track of, especially as you implement all the important self-care tasks in this book from day to day. Be sure to manage your time so you can accomplish everything and not get overwhelmed. On the next pages are monthly and daily planners you can copy, or download from my website (https://wwwthegriefgirl.com /be-you--only-better.html), and use to get started. First, evaluate the entire month, noting the bigger projects or tasks at hand. Then zero in on weekly and daily goals in more detail.

MONTHLY PLANNER

| JAN | FEB | MAR | APR | MAY | JUN | JUL | AUG | SEP | OCT | NOV | DEC |

TOP GOALS

THINGS TO DO

NOTES

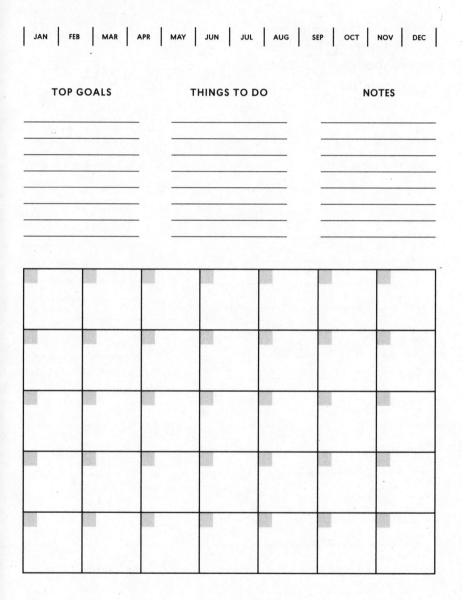

DAILY PLANNER

DATE

M TU W TH F SA SU

SCHEDULE

GOALS

| 6 AM |
| 7 AM |
| 8 AM |
| 9 AM |
| 10 AM |
| 11 AM |

TO DO

| NOON |
| 1 PM |
| 2 PM |
| 3 PM |
| 4 PM |
| 5 PM |
| 6 PM |
| 7 PM |
| 8 PM |

NOTES

| 9 PM |
| 10 PM |

CHAPTER 7

Manage Your Money

Josh's family always seemed to have enough money. His parents never said no when he asked them to pay for a school field trip, new shoes, or sports equipment. By the time he graduated high school, Josh was working part-time at an ice-cream shop, and his paychecks went toward fun — cool new clothes, movie and concert tickets, and eating out with friends.

Even during Josh's freshman year in college, his parents paid for nearly everything — tuition, books, rent, and groceries. But, after that year, when Josh decided to share an apartment with friends near campus rather than return home for the summer, his parents told him he'd have to get a job and pay his own rent and living expenses. That was fine with Josh — his buddy had already offered to get him a job in his father's landscaping business, and Josh figured that would be more than enough to keep him going all summer.

Only it wasn't. Sure, he knew he needed rent money — but that didn't seem like much compared to what he was making. And other than that, Josh hadn't really thought about what else he might need to budget for; in fact, budgeting never even crossed his mind.

When he got his first paycheck, Josh was disappointed — after all the taxes and deductions were taken out, it was much less than he'd anticipated. Still, it was money he'd earned himself, and he was proud of that. Over the weekend, he treated his friends to dinner, bought a new wakeboard for his next trip to the lake, and snagged the AirPods he'd had his eye on for months.

Later, when Josh's roommate asked him for his rent check, Josh wrote it without a second thought — until the check bounced and Josh's account was suddenly overdrawn. His roommate was irritated. Josh didn't have the money to cover the bounced check and the overdraft fees, he didn't want to call his parents, and his next payday was still a week away.

That day on his way home from work, he noticed a sign that read, "Short on cash? Come in for a payday advance." Josh pulled in, figuring it was the easiest way to get his rent paid and some money in his pocket for the coming week. He'd pay it right back and be more careful over the next few weeks.

But when Josh paid the loan back, it cost him 25 percent in interest. Plus, he'd already lost money paying his overdraft fees. Even though it was payday, he felt like he was practically in the hole again. That night, his friends were headed to a baseball game and Josh didn't want to miss out, even though the tickets were expensive. He decided he'd go, reassuring himself that if he came up short again, he'd get a payday loan *just one more time*, then start being more careful.

Despite his best intentions, getting payday advances became a habitual cycle that was tough to break — after all, he was always practically broke by the time he paid the last loan off on payday. Josh started feeling stressed-out all the time. He felt guilty when he bought new things or spent too much eating out, but he couldn't seem to resist the temptation, either.

Then one week, Josh came down with the flu. There was no way he could work in the sun all day, so he called in sick — then again the next day, and the next, and the next. He missed almost an entire week before he felt better, and his job didn't offer sick pay or vacation time. That week, his paycheck was half of what it usually was, and he didn't have anything saved to cover the payday loan he'd taken out two weeks before. He extended the loan at an even higher interest rate, not knowing whether he'd have the money to pay it back in two weeks. Plus, his rent was due, and his fridge was practically empty.

Josh needed help. He finally called his dad and told him he needed money. His dad asked what was going on with his job, and Josh admitted he'd been living not just paycheck to paycheck but one paycheck *behind* and had been for a couple months, while shelling out most of his earnings to pay the interest on his short-term loans.

Josh's dad didn't offer him money, but he did take him to lunch to talk about his finances. When he asked if Josh had ever made a budget, Josh sheepishly told him no; he didn't have many expenses and figured it'd all work out. Josh's father pulled a laptop out of his briefcase and opened a spreadsheet. He asked Josh to list everything he'd spent money on the previous month — whether necessary or not.

When Josh saw how much he'd actually been spending on things like fast food and iced coffees, he couldn't believe it — the small amounts felt so nominal on a daily basis, but by the end of the month, it was more than he spent on rent. Meanwhile, the fresh groceries he'd purchased were going bad in the refrigerator.

Together, Josh and his father worked out a budget, taking into account his average paycheck, minus his rent, utilities, cell phone bill, car insurance payments, and gas. Josh designated 15 percent of his income for savings, leaving him with a comfortable weekly stipend for groceries, eating out, and occasional new clothes or event tickets. If Josh could stick to the budget, he wouldn't need a payday loan again. Josh's father generously offered to loan him the money to pay off his current short-term loan, and Josh worked a weekly payment into his budget so he could pay his father back within a couple of months.

The thought of a budget had always felt stifling to Josh — but after the stress and anxiety of the previous months, it was the exact opposite. He spent money without feeling guilty — after all, he knew if he stuck to his daily budget, he'd have the money he needed to cover all his expenses. And by steadily putting money into a savings account, he knew he didn't have to worry about emergency situations like getting sick and missing work.

Managing his money successfully gave Josh confidence he'd never had before; he started to feel like a genuinely responsible adult. When school started in the fall, he carefully planned his schedule so he could keep his job part-time.

His parents still helped with his tuition and educational expenses, but Josh felt more independent all the time — and he loved seeing his savings account grow. He didn't have plans for the money, but knowing it was there gave him peace of mind. Though he never would have thought living on a budget could make him happier, that's exactly what it did — all it took was a little planning and discipline. While neither of those seemed easy at first, as he practiced, they came more naturally — as did the confidence of financial independence.

Budgeting Is Self-Care

Whether or not you currently have a credit card, savings account, student loans, or even a job, money management is a skill you need to develop. Maybe it's surprising that a book on self-care devotes a chapter to financial organization — that is, until you consider the consequences of financial *dis*organization. Like the payday loans Josh struggled with, credit-card debt can become a slippery slope, leading to payments that are hard to keep up with and creating exponential problems as interest on unpaid balances accrues and ends up costing more than whatever was bought in the first place. Further, money management is not always taught in high school or college, leaving many young adults with no idea how to manage their money, get out of debt, or apply for credit. This is unfortunate, as teenagers and young adults are more than capable of handling basic financial responsibilities. In fact, a 2015 *Journal of Consumer Affairs* article asserts that children as young as age five are developmentally capable of saving money.

As young people learn to save money and manage their personal finances, they gain real-world decision-making skills they can use in all aspects of their lives. Additionally, if you're fortunate to learn basic financial responsibility while still living with your parents or other caregivers, you can learn from any mistakes you make (which are inevitable) while guided by their advice and surrounded by the "safety net" they provide.

Of course, not everyone has that safety net — even when they do live with their parents. Ultimately, however, money management is an important skill for *everyone*, no matter what their circumstances are, learning the basics now — including budgeting, saving, spending, building and using credit, and making wise investments — can set you up for financial success for years to come.

By responsibly managing your finances, you build your self-confidence while reducing stress and anxiety. Regardless of your life goals or ambitions, mismanaging money can wreak havoc on both your financial and mental health. Learning self-discipline and self-reliance pays dividends — literally! So build good money management habits now.

Managing Your Money

Whether you work full-time or part-time or depend on money from your parents, government grants, or scholarships, mastering these concepts of fiscal responsibility is essential to your financial and mental health.

Practice self-control and delayed gratification

It's never fun to deprive yourself of something you want or to miss out on a cool event. But controlling your finances — rather than allowing them to control you — often involves practicing self-control and delayed gratification. The best and easiest way to do both is to only buy what you can pay for with the cash you already have on hand. Then, if you use a credit card for purchases, you can pay off the entire balance with every bill. Sounds simple, and it is, but in practice, what it often means is waiting to buy what you want until you can actually afford the purchase. This delay gives you time to consider the purchase: Is it something you really need, or is it an impulse buy? Credit cards make it easy and convenient to spend much more than you earn, but that debt can hang over your head for years — and the last thing you want is to still be paying for impulse items five or ten years from now.

In addition, there are numerous money-sending apps like Venmo, PayPal, and Zelle, among others. Use them sparingly and only when you know you have enough money in your account to spend it.

Take charge of your education

Some parents teach their kids financial literacy — and some don't. Maybe you already know how to budget, apply for a credit card, and use a checking account — and maybe you don't. If not, instead of relying on others for advice, read up on personal money management or take a course through a local college. There are numerous classes and resources available, both online and in person — many of them free of charge.

Live within your means

It's tempting to want to experience all the great things in life — even if you can't afford them. But when your expenses exceed your income, life becomes stressful and filled with anxiety — anything but enjoyable. That's why it's important to set a budget and track your spending. You might find, like Josh did, that those daily mocha lattes from Starbucks are keeping you from building a nest egg that will empower you later. Use apps or software — many of which are free — to track your income and keep tabs on your spending. That way, you can see where you might be overspending and where you might be able to save money or pay down debt.

Start or keep saving

If you haven't already, develop the habit of regularly saving money, which will serve you throughout your life. Each month, set a savings goal, such as trying to save 20 percent of your income — or however much you can afford — and keep that money in a separate savings account. Let it build; don't touch it. At first, this money can serve as an emergency fund, but eventually it can help you afford life's larger purchases when you need or want them — such as buying a new car or new furniture, taking a dream vacation, moving into a new apartment, or making a down payment on a home.

Invest in your health

If you're young and healthy, it's easy to underestimate the importance of having health insurance. But not only is health insurance a must to keep you mentally and physically well — it's also the law. Without insurance, if and when you need to go to the emergency room for an accident — or even a bad flu — you could be on the hook for thousands of dollars in medical bills. Plus, with good health insurance, you're more likely to get preventative care, which will keep you healthier — and reduce the need for expensive treatments down the line.

Purchase quality over quantity

Become a good consumer by taking the time to research purchases to make sure you're buying a product that will last — at a good price. When you buy quality items at a good price, you'll spend less in the long run.

Use credit as a tool

Credit cards aren't just a scheme to get us to purchase things we can't afford so we wind up paying double through interest payments. They have some genuine benefits. One is that using and regularly paying off credit cards is a way to help build a good credit history, which banks use when considering people for car and house loans. Many credit cards also have points programs redeemable for airline travel, cash, and other goods. And so long as you pay off your entire credit-card bill every month, you won't pay unnecessary interest.

Avoid emotional spending

In the moment, impulse buying can feel good — but getting yourself into a precarious financial situation certainly does not. Recognize your triggers for emotional spending — like stress, boredom, desire to celebrate, or a bad day or bad mood — when you're tempted to buy something as a pick-me-up. By better understanding your behavior, you can stop yourself from reckless spending and find healthier, cheaper alternatives if your mood needs a boost, like exercise or spending time with family and friends.

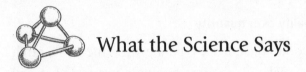 ## What the Science Says

Money affects your brain.

Money and your brain have a complex relationship, and having too little money actually has adverse effects on the brain. In a study on how income affects the brain, researchers found that having less money can actually impact thinking and memory by affecting the brain's gray matter and neural network organization. Researchers found that those with enough money had more gray matter and more segregation in the networks, which means that the different regions of the brain, such as those controlling speech and bodily functions, are able to function better because they overlap less. Another potential effect of money on the brain is that the pursuit of wealth can become addictive. Like gambling or compulsive shopping, this is an addiction to a process, not a chemical (such as cocaine or nicotine). But it produces a similar release of dopamine that the brain comes to depend on, and it can be just as destructive.

Money affects your sense of well-being

The relationship between money and our sense of well-being is complicated. Having more money increases our subjective well-being, but only up to a point, which one study calculated as an income of $75,000 per household. Having more money beyond that amount did not yield greater well-being. In addition, well-being is affected by how we spend money. Research suggests that inexpensive, everyday pleasures, like buying a favorite drink and sitting on a beach, may actually predict happiness more than winning a lottery!

Essentially, research suggests that well-being increases when we can provide ourselves with our essential needs and experiences, and less so when we purchase expensive material goods. In fact, greater materialism is associated with lower self-esteem and less compassion for others. Having far more money than you need can isolate you, make you less helpful and empathetic, and stress you out.

Your financial health affects your physical health

Studies have concluded that financial stress influences our physical health. Economic hardships are associated with increased pain, lower pain tolerance, and an increased risk of heart disease. The American Psychological Association considers financial stress to be one of the top childhood adversities, right up there with abuse, neglect, and a dysfunctional household, all of which negatively impact physical health.

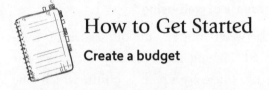

How to Get Started

Create a budget

Relieve stress and see the big picture of possibilities with a clear budget. On the next page is a worksheet you can use to create and keep track of your monthly budget, which will help you achieve the financial freedom you are looking for. You can make blank copies from this book, or download and print it from my website: https://www.thegriefgirl.com /be-you--only-better.html. You may also wish to try out budgeting software, a budgeting app, or online resources from your bank. The important thing is to create a budget, stick to it, and adjust it periodically to reflect any changes in your income, expenses, or lifestyle.

Remember to budget for special outings and self-care, which will help you follow through with your financial plan.

BUDGET WORKSHEET Month: _____ 20__

Primary Income	Other Income	Total Income
+	**=**	

Fixed Expenses / Bills	BUDGETED	ACTUAL
MORTGAGE/RENT		
HOME/RENTER'S INSURANCE		
CAR PAYMENT		
CAR INSURANCE		
PHONE		
INTERNET/CABLE		
ELECTRICITY		
HEATING		
WATER		
GARBAGE		
HEALTH INSURANCE		
MEMBERSHIPS (GYM, NETFLIX, ETC.)		
OTHER		
TOTAL		

Variable Expenses	BUDGETED	ACTUAL
GAS/ TRANSPORTATION		
GROCERIES		
EATING OUT		
ENTERTAINMENT/ TRAVEL		
PERSONAL CARE (COSMETICS, HAIRCUTS, ETC.)		
PET CARE		
CLOTHES		
GIFTS		
CHARITY		
MEDICAL/DENTAL		
OTHER		
TOTAL		

Debt and Savings*	BUDGETED	ACTUAL

Monthly Totals		BUDGETED	ACTUAL
TOTAL INCOME			
FIXED EXPENSES	▬		
VARIABLE EXPENSES	▬		
DEBT	▬		
SAVINGS	▬		
TOTAL LEFT OVER	▬		

* In this section, list all debt payments (student loans, credit cards, etc.) and savings goals.

CHAPTER 8

Have Healthy Relationships

Kelsey was a biology student at the University of New Mexico in Albuquerque, and only once she moved away from home did she realize how dysfunctional her family was. Sure, she knew her parents fought a lot when she was younger, and she grew up avoiding certain topics or conversations with her parents for fear of another monumental argument, but she also figured her family was normal — or at least they were "normally" dysfunctional.

But from the first day of freshman year, Kelsey's college roommate, Maya, helped her see things differently. Maya arrived on campus with both parents and a little brother in tow, who spent an hour helping her unpack boxes and hang clothing in the closet before they tearfully hugged and made plans for dinner that evening. Kelsey's mom had dropped her off in a hurry to get back for a social engagement and hadn't even seen her dorm room.

Kelsey noticed how Maya spoke to her parents — and how *often* she spoke to them! She told them things Kelsey would never dream of telling her mom and dad, like getting asked out on a date on her first day of school or finding out she didn't get the on-campus job she was hoping for. Maya's parents seemed to be always supportive and loving — even when they gave her honest advice or feedback on guys she was dating.

During the year, Kelsey started dating, too. Her boyfriend, Sam, was a pre-med student who played drums in a band. From the start, Kelsey knew she wasn't the most important thing in Sam's life — school and music always came first. But she thought if she lost weight, wore the right clothes, or maybe considered pre-med as a major, too, Sam would pay more attention to her. She attended every one of his band's performances, helped quiz him for tests, and left sweet, supportive notes for him tucked into his textbooks.

No matter what Kelsey did, Sam still seemed half-hearted about her — and in turn, Kelsey often felt bad about herself when she was around him. Early in their relationship, Sam pressured Kelsey to have sex before she was ready, but she did it anyway, hoping it would bring them closer. Instead, Kelsey came to feel like sex was the only thing Sam wanted from her. At a party, if Sam handed her punch spiked with grain alcohol or a joint, she took it. Then she would spend the rest of the party either talking too much or stoned and paranoid, and in the morning, she'd feel regret and shame.

Sometimes Sam canceled their weekend plans at the last minute, and Kelsey would feel abandoned. She would visit Old Town by herself, stroll into artisan shops, and maybe buy herself a pair of earrings or eat lunch at a café, the whole time feeling lonely and sad.

The biggest bright spot was Kelsey's friendship with

Maya — in fact, they became close confidantes and told each other everything about their respective relationships. Maya's new boyfriend, Colton, was crazy about her — and the feeling seemed mutual. They took turns helping each other study, brought each other meals if the other was studying late, and encouraged each other in everything they did. They didn't drink and went on hikes in their free time.

One night, Kelsey came home in tears after Sam invited her over, slept with her, and then said he had to leave to meet with his band. Maya asked Colton if he would mind heading home early so she could be there for her friend. Colton agreed and gave Kelsey a warm hug on his way out. As Kelsey cried, she told Maya the things she'd never said to anyone.

"I'm just never good enough," she sobbed. "I was never good enough for my parents to pay any attention to unless they were yelling at me, and now I can't even keep my boyfriend interested in me for anything besides sex."

Maya listened thoughtfully. "Have you ever told your parents how you feel?" she asked. Kelsey said she hadn't. Why would she?

"Don't you think maybe you're choosing an unhealthy relationship because it's all you know?" Maya asked gently. Kelsey had never thought of it like that, but her relationship with Sam was a lot like her relationship with her parents — for one, she was always trying to get their attention or approval, and if that didn't work, she'd do something just to get an emotional reaction from them.

Maya and Kelsey talked most of the night, and in the morning, Kelsey made an appointment to talk to an on-campus therapist. Kelsey was hopeful that she could form healthy romantic relationships and avoid the constant dysfunction she grew up around.

Of course, she'd already had success in one important relationship — her friendship with Maya. Their friendship became even deeper as they communicated honestly and listened without judgment. Maya encouraged Kelsey to follow her therapist's advice and speak candidly with her parents. Through therapy, Kelsey saw that her choice of a neglectful romantic partner echoed the pattern she grew up with in her family, and Kelsey broke things off with Sam for good. In fact, making that decision was easier than she thought, especially with the support of a good friend like Maya.

Now, Kelsey hoped to improve her relationship with her parents, so that someday she might get the same kind of loving support from them as from her friend.

Strong Relationships Are Part of Self-Care

Building strong relationships takes work, but they are essential to our health and well-being. Creating a loving, supportive community of family and friends is a vital part of self-care. This might sound obvious, but it's worth reflecting on how important healthy relationships are and how to distinguish them from unhealthy relationships. In fact, relationships can affect our health just as much as sleep, diet, and smoking, according to Harvard Women's Health Watch. One study reported that a lack of strong relationships increased the risk of premature death from all causes by 50 percent!

Of course, living longer isn't the only reason healthy

relationships are important. They make life much more pleasurable and fulfilling. On the flip side, when relationships are unhealthy, they can harm our mental, emotional, and physical health. Unhealthy relationships can cause or exacerbate depression and anxiety and undermine confidence and self-esteem.

While relationships can be complicated — especially with family members and significant others — you can tell whether your relationships are healthy or unhealthy by checking in with yourself about how you feel when you're around someone. Paying attention to these signs and recognizing your own feelings can help you create positive, healthy, and lasting relationships — and address those that are not.

Healthy relationships are characterized by mutual affinity, trust, and respect. You enjoy spending time with the person, but are comfortable being apart when either of you needs or wants space. You don't feel a need to change your personality, appearance, or beliefs to gain the person's approval, and you both support and encourage each other's other relationships. You also feel good about yourself when around this person, and you trust them to have your back — even when you're not around. When there is conflict, which happens in every relationship, you both can resolve it fairly, respectfully, and rationally, without feeling out of control or fearful for your safety. Lastly, you're honest with each other about what you think and feel, you respect each other's opinions and feelings, and you help each other equally.

Unhealthy relationships are characterized by the opposite of these things. You may feel competitive with, rather than supportive of, the other person. You may feel bad about yourself when around them or feel the need to change or hide things about yourself to gain their approval; you may do things that compromise your ethics to please them. You may fear they will gossip about you behind your back, and you may even fear violence and not feel safe. They may not be supportive of your other relationships. In unhealthy relationships, you may feel like you give more than you receive and that the other person doesn't support your goals and activities.

Relationships are always a two-way street. Both people are involved and play a role in the health of the relationship. However, you can learn a lot about the quality of your connections by how *you* feel. Pay close attention when you're around other people; check in with yourself and stay tuned in to your feelings. This is the first step to building healthier, long-lasting relationships and addressing those problems that may be dragging you down.

Let's talk about the various relationships in your life — with friends, family, romantic partners, and first and foremost, with yourself. All these relationships can affect your self-esteem, confidence, and happiness.

Self

Your relationship with yourself is the most important relationship there is. It lays the foundation for all your other relationships. If you do not treat yourself with respect and kindness, you won't do the same for others, and you will not attract people in your life who are healthy for you. You need to listen to yourself and not ignore or deny your own inner wisdom or intuition. If you feel peer pressure to behave in ways that feel wrong or destructive to you, you need to listen to and respect your inner voice. This might mean refusing to do drugs or drink alcohol if you don't want to, or it might mean offering compassion to someone whom others have rejected or shunned. Listen to your conscience.

If the foundation of all relationships is love, this is equally true with ourselves. Practice self-love. Forgive yourself when you fail, and be empathetic and nurturing with your painful feelings. If you feel the need to avoid or escape difficult emotions, acknowledge that with compassion, and give yourself a break, but avoid bad choices that will only make you feel worse. Commit to yourself for life because that's how long the relationship lasts.

When you have a healthy relationship with yourself, the other positive relationships in your life will grow and thrive.

Friends

Your friendships matter — a lot. Friendships play an important role in warding off depression and improving mental health. Having a friendship network also provides a sense of belonging, which in turn helps you feel more positive and confident.

It may not seem this way now, but life is not a popularity contest. The strength of your friendships is *much* more important than the number of friends you have. A few deep, close friendships are far more beneficial than dozens of superficial or unhealthy friendships.

When we fail a test, break up with a partner, or lose a job, we reach out to friends for consolation. We need relationships with people our own age, who are experiencing the same things we are, which helps us feel understood and supported.

Believe it or not, the friendships we make as young adults tend to be the strongest of our lives. A 2019 *Wall Street Journal* article reported that the twenties — often a time of important "first" experiences — are also the prime years for forming lifelong friendships. Why? Perhaps because these are the people who were with us and helped us as we discovered who we are and gained the confidence and integrity to be true to ourselves.

Choose friends who are supportive, empathetic, and respectful of your boundaries. A good friend should make you feel more confident and in control — not less. Build trust and loyalty by being a good listener and keeping private conversations confidential. Be true to who you are, but respectful of who your friends are, too.

Family

Our first relationships in life are, most often, with our parents and siblings — and those relationships can affect us for the rest of our lives. These are our first lessons in relationships, which shape what we expect and how we act in all our other relationships. For example, if parents are loving, kind, supportive, and understanding, children are more likely to seek and cultivate those qualities in their friendships and to view marriage, parenting, and family life positively. In dysfunctional families, such as when parents withhold love or are neglectful, children can struggle to recognize and foster healthy, fulfilling relationships with others.

Take Kelsey, for instance. Her experiences with her family growing up made it more difficult for her to trust other people and to create healthy and honest relationships, which led to her allowing her boyfriend, Sam, to neglect her. Of course, just because someone's family life growing up was less than idyllic doesn't mean they will fail at relationships — far from it! What's important is to recognize any familial dysfunction in order to set and maintain boundaries in those relationships, and then to foster healthier behaviors in other relationships. Remember, parents and siblings are not the only role models; we can learn from and emulate other significant adults in our lives, those who may have provided the safety and security we needed as children. Ultimately, whatever one's upbringing, everyone can learn how to build healthier, long-lasting connections.

That said, if you feel like your relationship with a parent or other family member is unhealthy, and you're unsure how to improve it or cope with it, you may want to talk to a professional family therapist, like Kelsey did. Addressing unhealthy relationships with family members can be much more complicated than resolving issues with friends. To find someone to talk to, consult your health insurance or school counselor, or ask friends for recommendations. A therapist can give you objective advice and help you manage and understand complex relationships.

As always, it's important to recognize your own feelings when engaging with anyone, but especially family members. Check in with yourself often and recognize your feelings in the moment; these will provide insight to help you understand and improve the relationship.

Romantic relationships

Exploring romantic relationships is an exciting part of being a young adult. So what's the best way to make a current romantic relationship and any future ones healthier? Get to know *yourself* better. In young adults, the emotional part of the brain is much more active than the logical/rational part. This means that when something highly emotional happens — like romantic or sexual feelings — it can be *really* hard to make logical, safe, healthy decisions.

So, the better you know yourself, the more capable you'll be of making better decisions in the moment. For instance, if a relationship ever makes you feel pressured to change yourself, to do something you wouldn't normally do, or to ignore your boundaries, you'll be able to recognize that the situation isn't healthy, and to respond in a way that's true to yourself.

Romantic relationships — like any in life — should make you feel better about yourself, increase your confidence, and motivate you to accomplish your goals and dreams. As you check in with yourself, take note if you feel uncomfortable, negatively pressured, or just plain bad about yourself. If you're feeling this way often, it could mean your relationship isn't healthy.

Time to Check In

How are you feeling right now? Name or label any emotions, positive or negative. If an emotion is negative, naming it will reduce its intensity.

Build Better Relationships

You could say life is made up of relationships. Building positive connections is much easier when you're practicing positivity in general. Be sure to read this book's chapters on mindfulness and gratitude — being present and being grateful are two ways you can strengthen your connection with yourself, others, and everything around you.

That said, strong relationships aren't built overnight — but you can start to build them *now*. Whether you want to improve an existing relationship or to put your best foot forward when forming new ones, here are some important ways you can build stronger, healthier connections in your life.

Be a good listener

Communication is at the heart of all relationships, and effective communication requires active listening, which means staying focused on what someone is telling you, rather than responding by telling them about yourself. For example, if your friend tells you "Ugh, I had a terrible day today," instead of responding with "Me, too!" and then listing everything that was bad about your day, you might say, "I'm sorry to hear that! What happened?" and then listen compassionately with your full attention. When you're *really* listening, you're more likely to better understand your friend, family member, or significant other and to make them feel supported.

Be giving, but set boundaries

Good relationships require sacrifice on both ends. Be willing to give your time and attention, but not to the point you feel taken advantage of. Healthy relationships require you to set and respect boundaries. If someone is asking too much of you — in terms of your time or emotions — or asking you to do something you're uncomfortable with, you need to be open and honest about those feelings.

Practice empathy

Empathy builds connections because people remember how you make them feel. Acting with empathy requires you to listen and understand while withholding judgment. Empathy puts you in another person's shoes, making it easier for you to comfort, advise, and relate.

Be present

There's nothing worse than pouring your heart out to someone who can't pull their eyes off their smartphone. Be present for the *people* in your life, not just the experiences. Any time you spend with a friend, family member, or significant other is an opportunity to nurture your relationship. Treat it as such.

Be honest

Healthy relationships require honesty because they're built on mutual trust. If you are honest about who you are, how you feel, and what you believe, you will build the trust you need for a lasting relationship.

Work through disagreements

Everyone is different, and every lasting relationship will have its arguments or disagreements. How you address these is what's important. When a disagreement happens, listen to the other person with the goal of understanding — not winning the argument. Rather than shutting down or avoiding speaking, open up about how you're feeling, even if you don't understand it yourself.

 # What the Science Says

Love affects your brain

When you fall in love, you turn on the pleasure center of your brain, stimulating dopamine production, but at the same time your serotonin level drops. This affects the prefrontal cortex, which is associated with the executive functioning of the brain and the modulation of emotions. This phenomenon is why "falling in love" can make you a little crazy and why you may not be thinking as reasonably as usual. However, over time the serotonin production returns to normal, and long-lasting relationships increase oxytocin, the neurotransmitter associated with feeling calm and nurtured.

Healthy relationships make you happier

It's been proven that a lack of social ties is linked to depression. Humans are social animals, and we do not do well in isolation. Studies have shown that the elderly, for example, live longer and more fulfilling lives if they engage in relationships. They are also less likely to suffer from dementia. Studies have also shown that positive family relationships during adolescence may reduce the risk of depression in midlife.

Healthy relationships are good for your physical health

Healthy relationships have many benefits for the body. Most of them are linked to the reduction of cortisol, which is a stress hormone that can throw your whole body out of balance. Stress can adversely affect your coronary arteries, gut function, insulin regulation, and immune system. Social ties also help control blood pressure and are associated with having a healthy body mass index (BMI).

Relationships thrive with kindness

This may not sound scientific, but relationships that thrive do so because of attentiveness and kindness — and not only when the going gets tough, but when things are going well, too. One study asked young-adult couples to talk about recent positive events in their lives, and then studied their responses. Some people ignored their partner, some acknowledged them half-heartedly, some changed the subject, and some diminished the news. Others displayed an "active constructive response" — in other words, the partner engaged wholeheartedly with enthusiasm. This was found to be a marker for the relationships that lasted longer, since these couples stayed together. So in relationships, kindness and turning toward your partner make the relationship more likely to succeed, in both good times and bad.

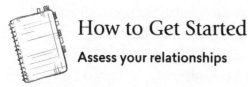

How to Get Started

Assess your relationships

Using the suggestions below, take some time to write about and evaluate your relationships, along with what you feel you do well and not as well to build healthy relationships. You'll consider why you might get along effortlessly with some people but be in frequent conflict with others. Are there patterns? Remember, whenever you consider how to fix any relationship issues, the best place to start is within yourself.

- First, in a journal or notebook, list the people in your life that you have a close relationship with.
- In that list, note any relationships that have unhealthy characteristics, and what those are. For example, note if you don't always feel safe or trust a certain person, and for what reason. If someone isn't always supportive, or if being with them brings you down, specify how.
- Next, note relationships in your list that have healthy characteristics and what those are (even if those relationships also have negative aspects). For example, note relationships in which you feel safe or that lift you up, encourage you, and motivate you.
- Compare the healthy and unhealthy characteristics. How do they make you feel? Do you notice any connections among them?
- Finally, consider yourself and how you are in relationships. Make a list of times in the past when you

have displayed positive relationship qualities and helped those closest to you: When were you supportive? When did you lift someone up? When were you reliable? Then consider:

How can I be kinder?
How can I be a better friend?
How can I be a better listener?

CHAPTER 9

Be Mindful

"Damon, you're scaring me," said Damon's girl-friend, Lydia.

He had just ripped a picket off his fence and yelled in rage because he'd gotten a parking ticket, again. He knew getting the ticket had been his own fault, and he was angry and upset, mostly at himself. He set the broken picket on the ground and wiped the sweat off his forehead. He felt a wave of sadness. He loved Lydia and didn't want to scare her.

"I'm sorry," he said.

Damon had a temper, and he was impulsive and often not present. He and Lydia frequently fought because he would blurt out hurtful things without thinking. He would also send angry emails he'd later regret and eat so much junk food he felt sick. But for Damon, this day became the final straw.

Damon lived in South Bend, Indiana, and his parents fought all the time and were on the brink of divorce. It was summer, and while Lydia was going to Indiana University in Bloomington in the fall, he'd decided to take a gap year.

The uncertainty of his future was making him anxious. He didn't even know if he'd keep living with his parents. He felt pressure to figure out his life, but he needed time. He had no idea what he would study once he went to college.

Damon looked up at Lydia, at her brown curls and wide eyes. "I'm sorry, I really am."

That evening he searched online for information on how to be less impulsive and how to control anger. He found a site about mindfulness. It said that if you pause before you act and center yourself, you'll act with more awareness. It also suggested meditation, so Damon set down the phone, closed his eyes, and tried it. At first his thoughts were overwhelming and heightened his anxiety, but he kept fantasizing that he was breathing them out. Damon only had patience to practice for five minutes, but afterward, he felt calmer and more centered.

The site said just five minutes a day could make a difference, so Damon practiced meditating every evening. He also made himself pause more before he spoke or ate, and he made an effort to be kinder. He began to have more faith that with time and calm attention, his life path would become clear. He started reading psychology books and thought about studying to be a psychologist. Damon took charge of his own responses and became a witness to himself.

One day he and Lydia were sitting under an oak tree in his yard and watching his pet turtle, Felix, move slowly across the lawn.

Lydia laughed and said, "Turtles are so slow."

Damon picked Felix up and put him on his lap. "There's really no rush, though, is there?"

Mindfulness Is Self-Awareness

Through the simple task of slowing down and checking in with himself, Damon was able to make changes in his life that improved his well-being. This is what I urge you to do while reading this book with each "Time to Check In" box: to pause and become aware of how you feel and what you need in this moment.

That's really what mindfulness is all about, self-awareness. Mindfulness is the ability to be and stay aware of your experiences and feelings in the present moment, including your physical, mental, and emotional needs. Practicing mindfulness requires an attitude of nonreactivity, but this doesn't mean doing nothing. On the contrary, being mindful means curbing seemingly automatic actions and reactions and instead thinking each one through. Mindfulness helps you respond, rather than react, to people and situations. When mindful, you are more likely to curb angry responses or unhealthy impulses. You will also be in touch with your emotions and feel them, acknowledge them, before you react.

When you live mindfully, you do what this book has encouraged you to do from the start — you pause to ask yourself questions like, "Am I sure I want to do this?" "Am I overreacting?" "What are the pros and cons of this choice?" and "What are the potential consequences of my actions?"

Of course, this doesn't mean you'll need ten minutes' lead time whenever you're required to act or respond; as you practice mindfulness, your awareness will naturally increase — and you won't need to remind yourself to check in. You'll just do it, especially as you learn to recognize strong emotions like fear, anger, and anxiety that trigger impulsive responses. The beauty of mindfulness is that it can decrease or even eliminate the sort of unthinking aggressive or defensive reactions we often later regret. Learning this skill as a young adult is important because your brain is still developing and wired to act impulsively.

Rather than living with the consequences of poor decisions, you can mindfully embrace your ability to consciously make rational decisions — even in the moment. Mindfulness increases self-awareness because it requires you to step back and think about each situation and your role in it.

Living mindfully and with intention also improves mental and physical health, overall well-being, and emotional intelligence. As you focus on living in the present, you will experience a reduction of stress and be less likely to feel stuck in past regret or paralyzed in worry and doubt. This frees your mind and emotions to connect better with those around you. Emotional intelligence is simply awareness of emotions, which helps you understand and manage your own emotions, reduce reactivity, and resolve disagreements and conflicts less emotionally and more effectively. It's the result of being empathetic and striving to understand other people better.

Emotional intelligence requires good communication between the rational, logical part of the brain (the prefrontal cortex) and the emotional part of the brain (the amygdala). Mindfulness is the bridge that connects these two areas, helping you acknowledge your feelings while finding rational solutions to any situation.

When emotions are highly charged, feelings of stress, anger, anxiety, and fear can take over. With mindfulness, and by developing your emotional intelligence, these feelings lose their power because you learn to respond intentionally, not impulsively. With consistent practice, mindfulness even builds new neural pathways in your brain that will become stronger and make this easier over time.

Practice Mindfulness

Here are some mindfulness practices that you can try.

Meditation

Creating a consistent meditation practice three to four times a week is a great way to practice mindfulness. By taking a moment to clear your mind and tune in to your breathing, you lower your blood pressure and stress levels, increase your ability to recognize your thoughts and emotions, and identify those that may be bringing you down or holding you back.

Find a quiet, comfortable space, relax, close your eyes, and take ten deep breaths. Pay attention as your breath goes in and out, notice when your mind wanders, and return it to your breath. This practice of returning to your breath keeps you intentionally in the present, anchoring you to the current moment.

If you're new to meditation, start by practicing for three to five minutes each session. Then increase your time gradually.

Affirmations

Affirmations are powerful positive statements that can be used over and over to help you find and maintain an upbeat, fulfilled mindset. They are generally in the present tense, as if the desired outcome has already happened. Here are a few examples:

I am doing well in school and getting good grades without feeling stressed-out.
I have plenty of money for everything I need.
I am loved by many people and have healthy relationships.

When you feel yourself mentally drifting away from the present, pause and repeat an affirmation. Say it three times, out loud, if possible, or in your mind, and then take three deep breaths. Notice how you feel when you finish.

Mindful walking

Mindful walking is a type of mindfulness practice. Either inside or outside, walk slowly while focusing on each step as you plant one foot and raise the other. Become aware of your entire body — how your leg lifts, your hips move, your arms swing, and your balance shifts. Do this for a few minutes, returning your awareness to your physical body if your mind wanders. Mindful walking increases your awareness of yourself and the world around you and keeps you from living on autopilot.

Writing

The practice of writing down your feelings pulls you into the present and allows you to analyze your thoughts and feelings on a deeper level. Create a consistent journaling practice, which is a healthy and safe form of expression. For more information on journaling, see "Build the Journaling Habit" (pages 15–16).

Acceptance

Practicing acceptance is much different than giving up. Acceptance means allowing yourself to feel every emotion that comes your way — sadness, anger, joy, confusion, apathy, fear — without guilt or judgment. Each emotion is part of you. As you recognize and feel all your emotions, you work toward accepting the real and complete you.

Intentional eating

Another mindfulness practice is to just eat without doing anything else. Don't "eat and…" or "eat while…" Make a conscious effort not to snack on the go, scarf your lunch in the car, or mindlessly nibble at your desk. Enjoy every bite; taste the food you're enjoying. Turn off the TV, put away your phone, sit down, and be fully present with your food. Be mindful of what your body needs in that moment, and be mindful of when your body is satisfied.

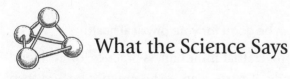 ## What the Science Says

Mindfulness affects your brain

According to studies, practicing mindfulness meditation causes beneficial changes in the brain. One study found changes in the concentration of gray matter in the areas of the brain associated with learning, memory, and emotion. Mindfulness activates several regions — the insula, associated with compassion and self-awareness; the putamen, associated with learning; the anterior cingulate cortex, which regulates blood pressure and heart rate; and the prefrontal cortex, where high-order learning occurs.

Mindfulness can help with depression and anxiety

Several studies have found that mindfulness can help combat depression and anxiety. One study showed mindfulness intervention lowered the relapse rates of people who have had three or more recurrent bouts of depression, though this was most effective for people with a history of trauma and abuse, and researchers cautioned this should be practiced in a therapeutic context. Another study asked participants to watch a disturbing film and found that the ones who practiced mindfulness were less reactive and anxious. It is also theorized that mindfulness is good for mental health because it breaks the cycle of self-rumination, the cause of negative self-talk. Instead of indulging in worries, with meditation you can connect to a still center within yourself and be more present in your environment.

Mindfulness can be good for your physical health

Studies have proven that mindfulness practice lowers blood pressure. A study of participants who practiced it and then took a six-minute walking test displayed improvement. A study on patients with HIV or breast cancer found that mindfulness appeared to help the immune system by increasing the levels of T-cells.

Mindfulness can help your eating habits and sleep

Mindfulness practice can lead to a healthier diet and to sleep improvement, which is not surprising when one considers how it affects your brain. If you are less reactive and if your prefrontal cortex is stimulated, you will make better decisions about your diet. In addition, if you regularly manage stress through mindfulness, you are more likely to sleep better.

Mindfulness can improve your relationships

Several studies suggest that mindfulness practice increases both relationship satisfaction and empathy. It makes you better able to respond to emotional stress and to express and acknowledge emotions, thereby improving relationships.

How to Get Started

Mindfulness prompts

What thoughts typically fill your mind? Deadlines, household tasks, the news, your future, social media? When your mind is full of unwanted buzz and negative thoughts, use mindfulness prompts to clear it and cultivate a positive mindset, focus your awareness on the present moment, and help you enjoy a much richer practice of living in the now.

Here are some ways to focus the time you spend sitting quietly in mindfulness, followed by prompts for writing about them in your journal. Feel free to adapt these to make them your own.

- Visualize an important goal and the steps you will take to achieve it.

  My goal:

  The steps I will take to achieve it:

- Reflect on the people in your life who love and support you and the reasons why.

  I feel grateful for _____ for supporting me by _____.

- Pay attention to each breath you take. Inhale through your nose and into your lungs, and exhale through your nose. Repeat this mindful breathing for several minutes.

  After doing this breathing practice, I notice that my body feels...

- Sit quietly for a few moments and watch your thoughts as they drift in your mind. Don't judge or respond to them; simply observe and acknowledge them.

  Observing my thoughts reveals these things about myself and how I feel today:

- As you meditate, notice your feelings without judging them. As emotions arise, give them names: "This is anxiety," "This is love," and so on.

  I noticed these feelings in myself while meditating:

- Reflect on spending time recently with someone you care for, when you felt mindful and engaged.

  This is how I spent my time with _____ and how I felt:

CHAPTER 10

Be Grateful

For Tanisha, life had never been "easy." Growing up in Tennessee, she witnessed her parents' frequent, explosive arguments until they divorced when she was ten, and she moved with her mother to Michigan. Tanisha had a hard time adjusting to a new city, the cold winters, and a new school, and she missed her father terribly. Her mom tried her best, but she was now single and working full-time, and she rarely had time to help Tanisha with homework or take her on fun outings. Tanisha frequently missed school and extracurricular events.

Plus, Tanisha was poor — or at least she felt that way. By the time she was in high school, most of the kids she knew had smartphones, and some even had their own cars. Tanisha started working as soon as she could. She got a low-paying job as a hostess at a local restaurant, and she spent her earnings on clothes and lunch, since her mom rarely had extra cash to give her. She had an old-model smartphone, but she had to pay the bill, and the broken screen embarrassed her.

Tanisha was a good student, but academic success didn't come naturally. Between school and work, her grades slipped her junior year, and she feared she wouldn't get into college — much less earn a scholarship, which she thought was the only way she'd be able to afford to go.

Junior year, when her first-semester grades were posted, Tanisha was devastated she'd earned a C in English. She felt like all the time she'd spent killing herself to study, work, walk to school, and keep her head above water was completely wasted. She was angry at her mother for not making more money, angry at her father for being out of the picture more than he was in it. She was angry that life seemed so easy for so many other kids. Everything felt hard for her.

One day while talking to her guidance counselor about her college plans, Tanisha broke down crying. She believed she didn't have a chance at college or success or happiness because of her parents' divorce, her move to another state, and her family's finances. To Tanisha's surprise, the counselor didn't brush her off *or* suggest she retake her class or look at local junior colleges.

Instead, she urged Tanisha to keep a gratitude journal, where she focused her energy on everything that was going *right* in her life — not what was going wrong. Skeptically, Tanisha followed the advice for a week. At first, she had to think hard to find the good in her life — like that the weather was nice that day or she got to have lunch with a friend at school. After a few days, it became easier. She started seeing blessings she'd never really thought about — that she was in excellent health, that she lived in a free country, and that her parents and grandparents were alive and loved her.

The next time she saw her counselor, Tanisha's attitude had shifted. She didn't cry over her laundry list of complaints and injustices. Instead, she focused on what was good in her life — and what she could change. Together, they identified various scholarships and grants for which she might be eligible. Tanisha told herself that even if none of these worked out, she'd find a way to get a great education and become a therapist herself, which had become her dream after her parents' divorce.

Shifting her focus to gratitude didn't change anything in Tanisha's life — but it also changed *everything*. Tanisha felt happier, which helped her feel more motivated. Keeping a gratitude journal became a habit she practiced every day. Through this, Tanisha realized that whatever her circumstances, there was always something to be grateful for.

Change Your Life by Changing Your Attitude

Tanisha was able to experience her life differently by changing her attitude and practicing gratitude. This simply means focusing on whatever is good in your life and feeling genuinely thankful for those things. People who practice gratitude pause to notice and appreciate things that others often take for granted. They make a point to reflect regularly on how fortunate they are when something good happens, and — more importantly — they do the same when something *bad* happens or when things don't go as well as they'd like.

Practicing gratitude trains you to look at life from a positive viewpoint and with the big picture always in mind.

It means recognizing the good in your life — both big things, like graduating college or making a sports team, and small, everyday things, like a good friend who's always there for you.

It's really hard to feel grateful without feeling good. And feeling good on a regular basis can have a big impact on your life. Positive emotions are good not only for your body and mind, but research shows that they are also good for your brain.

There are countless reasons why practicing gratitude is important. The first is that positive emotions have a domino effect. When you express gratitude toward someone else, you're likely to receive kindness in return, and a positive attitude often inspires positive actions in the people you interact with.

Next, when your attitude is based in gratitude, you learn better and make better decisions. That's because your positive mindset boosts your ability to absorb information and makes you more likely to think before taking action. As you learn and make better decisions, you grow — and personal growth produces positive emotions, continuing this cycle of happiness.

In addition, gratitude helps you "cancel" negative emotions. As you focus on gratitude and positivity, you transfer your energy to positive thoughts — rather than dwelling in negativity. This habit helps you reduce stress, combat anxiety, and increase happiness.

Gratitude also builds stronger relationships. As you recognize and share gratitude, you create personal bonds that are more loving, trusting, and healthy. Gratitude can transform your relationships with friends from competitive to encouraging and supportive.

Practicing gratitude helps you develop an instant form of happiness. Feeling grateful creates awareness of the good in your life in the present moment — a tool you can use for the rest of your life.

Feeling grateful doesn't always come naturally, but like mindfulness, it's a focus that anyone can cultivate. It's another way of learning how to regulate your emotions, and once you make gratitude a habit, this skill will stay with you for the rest of your life. Of course, when good things happen, we often feel gratitude spontaneously, and that's great. But to really access the power of gratitude, you need to deliberately count your blessings, rain or shine.

 ## Time to Check In

How long have you been sitting? Time to stand up and stretch.

Practice Gratitude

Here are some tips on how to easily foster gratitude in your life.

Slow down

To practice gratitude, start by actively taking in everything around you. Think about the simple things — the sounds in nature, the clouds in the sky. Take the time to thank people.

Smile at strangers. Pause to appreciate your surroundings, your friends, your family. Throughout the day, take a moment to think about what's good at *this* moment? Make an effort to focus on the small, everyday details you often overlook, and recognize what you may be taking for granted.

Start a gratitude board or journal

Like Tanisha, you may find that starting a gratitude journal is a great way to develop your own sense of gratitude. Make a habit of regularly devoting your journaling practice to writing down all the things you feel grateful for. Creating a gratitude board is another good technique. On a poster or corkboard, post sayings, pictures, and notes about the good things in your life, and keep this where you can see it every day. These practices help increase your awareness of the good in your life.

Create rituals

Establish a daily gratitude ritual: Start your day with positivity by expressing your gratitude — whether that's in a journal, out loud to yourself, or as a prayer. Notice what's good, and genuinely appreciate it — then absorb that feeling. Let it sink in. Savor your blessings in the moment they are happening.

Express your gratitude toward your loved ones

On a regular basis, tell the people in your life why you appreciate them and what they mean to you. This can be a simple "thank you" to your mom or roommate for a nice meal, or you can write a quick note or text to a friend who took the time to listen.

Be you

To cultivate gratitude for yourself, don't compare yourself to other people. There will always be someone more successful, intelligent, and athletic, if you choose to focus on that. Instead, focus on being the best version of you, rather than trying to match a standard set by someone else.

Speak and think positively

You're in control of your words *and* your thoughts. Start by using positive and enlightening words, which then helps you keep your thoughts positive. This concept applies to how you talk to *yourself*, too. Are you constantly self-critical? Do you treat yourself with the same respect you would give a trusted friend? When you speak positively to and about yourself, you become more positive — and that makes you a happier, more upbeat person to be around.

Adopt an abundance mindset

Happy people are content with what they already have, rather than focusing on what they lack. Resolve to become overwhelmingly positive about your life. This is possible because positivity is a choice. It's 100 percent up to you. See the good. Focus on the good. Expect the good. Receive the good.

Take a minute right now to stop and consider the good in your life. Now imagine how you would feel if you did that more often — or even constantly. As Tanisha experienced, feeling like you're destined for a life of problems does nothing to change the outcome — in fact, it probably makes a negative outcome much more likely.

As you gradually incorporate more and more gratitude in your daily life, it will change your outlook on life — which will then change your *life*. The habit of practicing gratitude and taking a positive view of your life is the fastest, simplest way to bring out the very best in yourself.

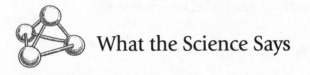 ## What the Science Says

Gratitude changes your brain

Feeling grateful stimulates the part of your brain that helps you retain information and make decisions. A 2017 study examined the effects of gratitude on adults who were in counseling for mental health concerns such as depression and anxiety. One-third of the participants were asked to write letters of gratitude, another third were asked to write about their negative feelings, and the remaining third did not do any writing activity. Those who wrote gratitude letters reported significantly improved mental health after four weeks. fMRI scans revealed that this group had enhanced activation in the prefrontal cortex, the area of the brain associated with learning and decision-making.

Gratitude is good for your body

Actively practicing gratitude has positive effects on your physical health. It makes your body stronger, healthier, and more resilient. It increases parasympathetic activity, which helps control stress and lowers blood pressure, as proven in a study of college students. Another study found that gratitude journaling intervention in seventy asymptomatic heart-failure patients improved heart function and decreased inflammation. In yet another study, it was shown to relieve pain and fatigue and boost energy levels for people with neuromuscular disease.

Gratitude improves your mental health

Numerous studies have shown that feelings and acts of gratitude improve well-being and alleviate depression. Gratitude frees you from negative emotions and replaces them with comforting and soothing thoughts. In one study of what's called the "three things exercise," participants wrote three things daily that they were grateful for, and the results showed marked improvements in depression. Appreciating what is valuable and meaningful to you makes you a happier person.

Gratitude improves your relationships

When you practice gratitude in your relationships, feelings of connection and satisfaction increase. Related to this is the fact that gratitude makes you more patient, according to a study from Northeastern University. When you practice gratitude, you are able to appreciate and see the good in people and in yourself. In addition, you are more tolerant and measured in your communication. This patience has a domino effect because focusing on gratitude changes your perspective of the other person, which in turn results in more positive communication, which then results in a more positive reaction by the other person.

Gratitude improves your sleep

You need to sleep — and sleep well — to feel good mentally and physically (as I discuss in chapter 2). So practice gratitude! It improves both sleep quality and sleep duration. Gratitude relaxes the nervous system and allows your mind to let go; it unshackles it from worries and negative thoughts that can keep you up at night.

How to Get Started

Practice gratitude

Maybe the best way to develop the habit of gratitude is to pause, whenever you think of it and wherever you are, and express gratitude for whatever occurs to you in that moment. You can also use any of the journaling prompts below. Your gratitude can be simple or deep. It's all about inspiration. Don't make it a burden. Mix it up each day, and focus on all the good that surrounds you.

- *I am grateful for...* [name anything — a smell, sight, taste, sound, memory, person, and so on].
- *I am looking forward to...* [name an event, be it tomorrow, next week, or next year].
- *A positive, unexpected, random surprise that happened today / this week / recently is...*
- *I feel grateful to* _____ [name a friend, colleague, family member, stranger], *and I will share my gratitude with them by...*

CHAPTER 11

Hope

Leah lived in Brooklyn with her mother and two older brothers. Her mother was a third-grade teacher. Her oldest brother worked at a restaurant as a waiter, and her other brother was always getting in trouble with the law and was on probation. Leah worked as an intern at a law firm with the dream of becoming a lawyer. But the job was tedious and unpaid. She filed documents and cleaned counters in the lunchroom. She wanted to be a lawyer, but it seemed like the goal was so much better than the steps to get there.

Once she went out to a bar with friends and stayed out late. While waiting on the subway platform to return home, she saw a homeless man missing a leg crumpled in a corner, and next to her stood a junkie with tracks on his arm. She looked at the dirty concrete floor and thought how the world was full of veterans with PTSD, species going extinct, absent fathers, and tedious jobs.

The next day she slept in and didn't show up for work. Her brother clattered dishes in the kitchen. It started snowing outside. Leah felt tired because she hadn't slept well. She'd kept waking up from a dream that she felt was important but couldn't remember, something about a dog that was sick. That's all she could remember.

There was a lot she couldn't remember. Her father had stopped visiting them when she was two years old, and all she had was a handful of pictures of him. Her mother said he moved to Arizona and worked on a ranch, that he'd always hated the city and that they always fought. Her brothers had a different father who sent them checks. She felt betrayed by the men in her life. Her last boyfriend had cheated on her with her best friend, and no decent men ever seemed to show interest in her.

She felt like a victim. The grief of the world and her despondency were one. Leah was depressed.

Every day she woke up determined to have a better day, to do better, to change her life, but the resolve was always gone by late morning. She felt guilt and shame about being late for work all the time and about her bad diet; she ate too much sugar. Most of all, she felt abandoned, even though she knew her mother loved her.

All winter long it snowed. The brownstones looked hard and accusing, the ice cruel. She was cold all the time. Her mother complained about not having enough textbooks at the school, her older brother was never around, and her other brother failed a drug test and was threatened with jail again.

One day at work a client came in crying; she was a housecleaner who was wrongfully accused of stealing jewelry. She had long gray hair, carried a bulky embroidered purse, and reminded Leah of her grandmother, who used to read her poems in the nursing home when Leah visited. Leah listened as the woman told her story to a lawyer: She had worked for the family for years and even knitted hats for their kids, and now they had turned on her. Leah thought of the poem her grandmother had read once, how hope was a thing with feathers. The lawyer listened and assured the woman he could help. Leah felt something lift inside. She realized that her job was actually supporting meaningful causes.

After that day, she paid more attention to the cases. She started paying attention to herself, too. She started showing up for work on time, eager to do her part. She also started paying more attention to what she was grateful for — her mother's love, her brothers' humor.

She began to see her resolve to be a lawyer not as an angry voice but as a hungry one. What if she nurtured and cared for it out of love, doing what she could in each moment, instead of treating it like an ideal she might never attain? What if she embraced the unknown?

She really didn't know what the future entailed, but she started making goals, and she started seeing that how she lived her life could lead toward a better future. Outside it still snowed, but she dressed warmly and waited for spring.

Hope Springs Eternal

Hope is the spring of all the seasons within you. For Leah, the shift to that season may not have happened right away, but eventually she was able to live her life in a way that fostered hope and had it as the foundation. Hope enabled her to make choices that were more mindful to honor and not abandon herself.

Hope is not just a fleeting moment or a temporary feeling that things will get better. It's a foundation for a lifestyle that reflects everything you do and everything you are. You can use hope to help motivate you to think positively and be proactive by making the most of every situation. Learning to manage your thoughts more effectively will help you respond in a healthy way, so nothing ever gets the best of you.

It's important to distinguish hope from resilience. Resilience is the ability to bounce back from a bad situation. If your house burns down or you experience other trauma, resilience is what enables you to survive it and move forward. Hope is often focused on specific goals. It's the positive conviction that by doing what you need to do — by filing the insurance claims, rebuilding, and taking stock — you will accomplish what you need to for a successful future. Indeed, it's the faith that with love and determination, you can overcome whatever challenges you face.

Hopeful people believe that everything in life is meaningful. When bad things happen, instead of feeling like victims, hopeful people accept what occurred and see the bigger picture and the part they are playing. They know that good often emerges from pain. This is different from blind optimism. Hope is pragmatic and practical; it guides someone to make the best, most effective choices. Hope is the belief that by making the best choices — by managing your money, fostering healthy relationships, managing your time, eating healthy, practicing mindfulness — you will improve your life and the world. You won't escape storms, but you will survive them and do better next time.

Hope is not necessarily something you are born with. You grow into it as you face adversity and choose to learn from your struggles. This positive mindset gives you the confidence to overcome your biggest fears and toughest challenges.

Time to Check In

List five takeaways you've gotten so far from reading this book. How will you change for the better?

Be Hopeful

Here are some ways to create a mindset of hope.

Be intentional

Overcoming fear is essential to developing a hopeful mindset. Take charge and know that it is within your control to become more hopeful. Think about what you need most in your life and then do it. It can be something as small as taking a break to go for a walk, taking a short nap, or reading your favorite book. When you take care of yourself even for a few minutes a day, these small moments accumulate and will change your attitude for the better.

Reflect and appreciate

Silently reflect on what you are grateful for, as I discuss in chapter 10. Take time every day to appreciate and feel a sense of connection to yourself and the world around you.

What if you were told today was the last day of your life?

How would you want to live it? Asking this question shifts our focus to who and what we are grateful for, and away from the daily petty annoyances that tend to grab our attention.

Reach out and help others

Do something good for someone else. Buy your friend a cup of coffee. Send someone flowers. Cook a meal for friends. Each time we make a difference in the lives of others, we create hope in ourselves and add more peace and hope to the world. Knowing this will give you hope.

Set goals

Goals help you focus on the positive outcomes you are working toward, instead of what you no longer have or what's not working for you. Your goals don't have to be accomplished all at once. Break them down into a series of small steps, and celebrate your successes along the way; this is the best way to keep yourself motivated. Start by prioritizing your top goals and move down the list to smaller ones. Remember, make sure your goals reflect what *you* want, not what your parents, teachers, peers, or employers expect.

Visualize success

Create a mental image of all the different paths you can explore to achieve your goals. Think of all the creative ways to overcome, rather than avoid, any obstacles you may face along your journey. Use positive self-talk and humor to learn to enjoy the process of attaining your goals. Visualize yourself achieving your goals. How do you feel? What are you grateful for? What have you learned? Who helped you along the way?

All of the self-care approaches discussed in this book are designed to help you trust and have faith in yourself. Know that you can get through any challenges that life throws your way. Developing healthy daily habits — which include mindfulness, journaling, moving, adequate sleep, gratitude, financial literacy, time management, enjoying nature, eating healthy, and asking for help when needed — provide the key ingredients for the most important aspect of self-care: hope.

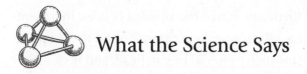 ## What the Science Says

Hope affects your brain

Having hope releases the brain's endorphins and enkephalins, hormones that promote well-being and help us handle stress. In addition, a study of 231 high school students revealed that the trait of hope relates to the orbitofrontal cortex, the part of the brain involved with reward, motivation, problem-solving, and behaviors associated with attaining goals.

Hope decreases anxiety and depression

The bottom line is that hope is associated with greater happiness. Many studies have measured hope's relationship to well-being. Hopelessness is more associated with suicide than depression! In one study, five hundred college students participated in a survey that measured their feelings of hope, depression, and anxiety. They repeated the survey months later, and the students who had expressed more hope had lower levels of depression and anxiety.

Hope is good for your physical health

The positive mood that hope instills is associated with numerous functions in the body: immune system response, cortisol profiles, and cardiovascular function. In fact, it's so good for your heart that it decreases your chance of death by heart attack or some other cardiovascular event. One study on cancer patients measured the amount of hope in patients after receiving a diagnosis. Researchers found that hope influenced the mortality rates of breast, head, and neck cancer patients, and improved outcomes in patients with AIDS. In another study, researchers surveyed eight hundred people between the ages of sixty-four and seventy-nine on their level of hope. Within four years, 29 percent of the people who defined themselves as hopeless had died, compared to 11 percent of those who said they were hopeful.

Hope can help you attain your goals

Hopefulness provides the motivation to achieve your goals. Evidence shows that hope is related to better academic, athletic, and occupational achievement. A study of eleven thousand employees in a variety of workplace environments revealed that hope accounted for 14 percent of employee productivity. In fact, it was shown to be a larger factor than intelligence or optimism.

Hope improves your self-esteem

When you are hopeful, you feel better about yourself. In studies on patients with or without hope, researchers have concluded that those who reported higher levels of hope and resilience also possessed higher self-esteem.

 ## How to Get Started
Find hope

Hope is embracing your authentic self. Look within and find your dreams. It's time to let hope shine. Answer the following questions in your journal to explore what hope means to you.

- What makes you feel joy?
- How do you envision your future?
- What choices can you make now to achieve your dreams?
- What are your fears?
- What action(s) can you take to overcome any fear or obstacles?
- Where or to whom can you go to get support?
- What are five ways in which you can share your most authentic self with the world?
    1.
    2.
    3.
    4.
    5.

Final Thoughts

After my husband, Bill, died, I wrote about how grief transformed me, and I began to have a vision of how I could better our world. I wanted to reach out to people who are young enough to make the kind of changes that ensure greater well-being. I saw how depression, anxiety, and other mental challenges were hurting our youth, and I wanted to make a difference so that nobody else would have to suffer like Bill did.

In your life, there will always be some suffering, and you can expect setbacks to your progress. Don't be an unforgiving perfectionist; be kind to yourself. You may vow to cut out sugar and then have a soda. You may misspeak in a relationship or miss a day of exercising. As with all healthy relationships, treat yourself with compassion, and listen to your inner voice as you build a solid foundation.

I think of all my self-care tips as a way to create a cocoon, an environment for your growth and transformation. I hope you write in your journal and take care of your body's health. I hope you are mindful of relationships and the beauty of nature and appreciate everything you encounter in your path. I want you to approach all you do and see with gratitude.

That includes being grateful for yourself. As much as this book is about making changes, it is also about making room for self-acceptance. It may seem like a paradox: In order to change, you must accept the person you are. But like most paradoxes, it is true. As the title of the book suggests: *Be You.*

If you build a home, the first task is to dig and pour the foundation. That foundation is hope. Your foundation of hope will inform the whole structure: the frame, the walls, the roof. Make changes with the intention to care about yourself, and wait. Spring, like hope, is just around the corner. Hope is not passive; it's active. The cocoon you are in is both a home and a waiting room where change takes place. When you emerge from it and engage with the world, you will take flight. You will be you...only better!

Photo credit: istock.com

Getting Help and
Mental Health Resources

By now, you've learned that self-care is about checking in with yourself regularly and learning to recognize and address your needs and emotions in the moment. With that in mind, one of the most important ways to practice self-care is to know when — and how — to ask for help.

Unfortunately, many people feel that asking for help — or even needing help in the first place — is a sign of weakness or an admittance of failure. That couldn't be further from the truth. In fact, asking for help shows both confidence in yourself and a commitment to living the healthiest, happiest life possible.

While many of the tactics in this book can help you identify and address your needs, you shouldn't ever feel like your physical, mental, and emotional health is all on you. You wouldn't try to cure yourself of cancer, so why try to suffer through something that a friend, family member, or trained professional could help with?

When and if you're facing something that seems insurmountable or unendurable, it's important to know where you can turn for help. The most obvious resource may be a parent, close friend, or family member. That's wonderful if you have that option, but not everyone does. If you don't know where to get help, or if you need more help than a friend or family member can provide, try the resources provided below. They are a great place to start. They contain a wealth of information and can connect you to professionals who are trained to help you.

After these resources, I've provided a blank Resource Contact List, which you can fill out with any resources that you know will help you, including others not listed here, such as a school therapist or local clinic. Feel free to tear out this page so you can keep this personalized Resource Contact List handy, or add any helpful contacts directly into your phone.

Mental Health and Suicide

IMALIVE
Online crisis intervention chat and information center
www.imalive.org

LGBT National Help Center
www.glbthotline.org
888-THE-GLNH (843-4564)

National Alliance on Mental Illness (NAMI)
www.nami.org
800-950-NAMI (6264)

National Hopeline Network
800-442-HOPE (4673)

National Runaway Safeline
www.1800runaway.org
800-RUNAWAY (786-2929)

National Suicide Prevention Lifeline
www.suicidepreventionlifeline.org
800-273-TALK (8255)

Teen Line
Teens helping teens
www.teenlineonline.org
800-TLC-TEEN (852-8336) or 310-855-HOPE (4673)
Or text TEEN to 839863

The Trevor Project
For gay and questioning youth in crisis
www.thetrevorproject.org
866-488-7386
Or text START to 678678

Drug and Alcohol Abuse

National Drug Helpline
www.drughelpline.org
844-289-0879

Substance Abuse and Mental Health Services Administration (SAMHSA)
www.samhsa.gov
800-662-HELP (4357)

Eating Disorders

National Association of Anorexia Nervosa and Associated Disorders (ANAD)
www.anad.org
630-577-1330

National Eating Disorders Association (NEDA)
www.nationaleatingdisorders.org
800-931-2237
Or text NEDA to 741741

Learning Disabilities and ADHD

Children and Adults with Attention-Deficit / Hyperactivity Disorder (CHADD)
www.chadd.org
866-200-8098

National Center for Learning Disabilities
www.ncld.org

ORGANIZATION:

PHONE:

WEBSITE:

NOTES:
_____
_____
_____
_____
_____

ORGANIZATION:

PHONE:

WEBSITE:

NOTES:
_____
_____
_____
_____
_____

ORGANIZATION:

PHONE:

WEBSITE:

NOTES:
_____
_____
_____
_____
_____

ORGANIZATION:

PHONE:

WEBSITE:

NOTES:
_____
_____
_____
_____
_____

ORGANIZATION:

PHONE:

WEBSITE:

NOTES:
_____
_____
_____
_____
_____

Endnotes

Introduction

p. 5   *Recent studies have shown that exercise is so effective*: Simon Young, "How to Increase Serotonin in the Human Brain without Drugs," *Journal of Psychiatry and Neuroscience* 32, no. 6 (November 2007), https://www.ncbi.nlm.nih.gov/pmc/articles/PMC2077351.

p. 6   *In one scientific study using brain scans, researchers compared*: Sonya McGilchrist, "Music 'Releases Mood-Enhancing Chemical in the Brain,'" *BBC News*, January 9, 2011, https://www.bbc.com/news/health-12135590.

Chapter 1: Write It Down

p. 16   *A UCLA study researched the effects on the brain*: "Putting Feelings into Words," *UCLA Today*, March 19, 2010, https://www.scn.ucla.edu/pdf/AL-UCLAToday.pdf.

p. 17   *According to the University of Rochester Medical Center, journaling*: "Journaling for Mental Health," Health Encyclopedia, University of Rochester Medical Center, https://www.urmc.rochester.edu/encyclopedia/content.aspx?ContentID=4552&ContentTypeID=1.

p. 17   *Research has shown that writing about negative emotions*: Siri Carpenter, "A New Reason for Keeping a Diary," *Monitor on Psychology* 32, no. 8 (September 2001), https://www.apa.org/monitor/sep01/keepdiary.

p. 17   *Journaling reduces stress, which has a fundamental impact*: These
details come from Joshua Smyth et al., "Online Positive Affect
Journaling in the Improvement of Mental Distress and Well-Being
in General Medical Patients with Elevated Anxiety Symptoms: A
Preliminary Randomized Controlled Trial," *JMIR Mental Health* 5,
no. 4 (October–December 2018), https://www.ncbi.nlm.nih.gov
/pmc/articles/PMC6305886; and F. Diane Barth, "Journaling Isn't
Just Good for Mental Health. It Might Also Help Your Physical
Health," *Think*, January 18, 2020, https://www.nbcnews.com/think
/opinion/journaling-isn-t-just-good-mental-health-it-might-also
-ncna1114571.

p. 18   *A study by psychology professor Dr. Gail Matthews discovered*: Ana
Juma, "7 Science-Based Benefits of Journaling," My Life Journal
(blog), May 10, 2019, https://mylifejournal.co/blogs/blog/7-science
-based-benefits-of-journaling.

Chapter 2: Get Good Sleep

p. 24   *According to* Neurology Live, *the shift in hormones*: Heidi Moawad,
"Teenage Circadian Rhythm," *Neurology Live*, November 7, 2016,
https://www.neurologylive.com/view/teenage-circadian-rhythm.

p. 26   *The National Sleep Foundation recommends 150 minutes*: "The Best
Exercises for Sleep," National Sleep Foundation, updated July 28,
2020, https://www.sleepfoundation.org/articles/best-exercises-sleep.

p. 27   *According to* U.S. News & World Report, *only 9 percent*: Heather
Monroe, "The Importance of Sleep for Teen Mental Health," *U.S.
News & World Report*, July 2, 2018, https://health.usnews.com
/health-care/for-better/articles/2018-07-02/the-importance-of
-sleep-for-teen-mental-health.

p. 27   *which should be from eight to ten hours a night*: "Sleep in Middle
and High School Students," Centers for Disease Control and
Prevention, updated February 5, 2018, https://www.cdc.gov
/features/students-sleep/index.html.

p. 27   *It is theorized that your brain can only get rid of the "toxic stuff"*:
Seung-Schik Yoo et al., "The Human Emotional Brain without
Sleep: A Prefrontal Amygdala Disconnect," *Current Biology* 17,
no. 20 (October 23, 2007), https://www.cell.com/fulltext/S0960
-9822(07)01783-6.

p. 27 *Research has shown that after just one week of sleep deprivation*: Rachel Leproult and Eve Van Cauter, "Effect of 1 Week of Sleep Restriction on Testosterone Levels in Young Healthy Men," *JAMA Network*, June 1, 2011, https://jamanetwork.com/journals/jama /fullarticle/1029127.

p. 28 *Decreased testosterone is associated with depression*: "Testosterone: What It Does and Doesn't Do," Harvard Health Publishing, Harvard Medical School, July 2015, https://www.health.harvard .edu/drugs-and-medications/testosterone--what-it-does-and -doesnt-do.

p. 28 *A lack of sleep decreases their production*: These details come from Eric Olson, "Lack of Sleep: Can It Make You Sick?" Mayo Clinic, November 28, 2018, https://www.mayoclinic.org/diseases -conditions/insomnia/expert-answers/lack-of-sleep/faq-20057757; and M. Irwin et al., "Partial Sleep Deprivation Reduces Natural Killer Cell Activity in Humans," *Psychosomatic Medicine* 56, no. 6 (November–December 1994), https://www.ncbi.nlm.nih.gov /pubmed/7871104.

p. 28 *An interesting scientific study among college students*: Stéphanie Mazza et al., "Relearn Faster and Retain Longer: Along with Practice, Sleep Makes Perfect," *Psychological Science* 27, no. 10 (August 16, 2016), https://journals.sagepub.com/doi/abs/10.1177 /0956797616659930.

Chapter 3: Get Up and Move

p. 38 *Exercise has numerous effects on the brain*: These details come from Brock Armstrong, "How Exercise Affects Your Brain," *Scientific American*, December 26, 2018, https://www.scientificamerican.com /article/how-exercise-affects-your-brain; and "Exercise and Mental Health," Health Direct, updated November 2019, https://www .healthdirect.gov.au/exercise-and-mental-health.

p. 39 *Because of these changes in your brain, exercise*: These details come from Sarah Gingell, "How Your Mental Health Reaps the Benefits of Exercise," *Psychology Today*, March 22, 2018, https://www.psychologytoday.com/us/blog/what-works-and -why/201803/how-your-mental-health-reaps-the-benefits -exercise; and "5 Mental Benefits of Exercise," Walden University,

https://www.waldenu.edu/online-bachelors-programs/bs-in
-psychology/resource/five-mental-benefits-of-exercise.

p. 39   *Regular aerobic exercise has also been shown to increase*: Heidi
Godman, "Regular Exercise Changes the Brain to Improve
Memory, Thinking Skills," Harvard Health Publishing, Harvard
Medical School, April 9, 2014, https://www.health.harvard.edu
/blog/regular-exercise-changes-brain-improve-memory-thinking
-skills-201404097110.

p. 39   *There are so many positive physical effects of exercise*: "Benefits of
Exercise," Medline Plus, updated July 27, 2020, https://medline
plus.gov/benefitsofexercise.html.

p. 40   *Exercise improves sleep by increasing your body temperature*:
"5 Mental Benefits," Walden University.

p. 40   *Exercise can make you feel more positive and confident*: Christina
Hibbert, "Exercise for Mental Health: 8 Keys to Get and Stay
Moving," National Alliance on Mental Illness, May 23, 2016,
https://www.nami.org/blogs/nami-blog/may-2016/exercise-for
-mental-health-8-keys-to-get-and-stay.

Chapter 4: Embrace Nature

p. 45   *In fact, scientists have found that spending two hours*: Mathew White
et al., "Spending at least 120 Minutes a Week in Nature Is Associated
with Good Health and Well-Being," *Scientific Reports* 9 (2019),
https://doi.org/10.1038/s41598-019-44097-3.

p. 47   *According to Harvard Health, a walk in nature decreases*: These
details come from "Sour Mood Getting You Down? Get Back to
Nature," Harvard Health Publishing, Harvard Medical School,
July 2018, https://www.health.harvard.edu/mind-and-mood/sour
-mood-getting-you-down-get-back-to-nature; and RaeJean
Boyd, "Evaluating the Role of Time Spent in Nature on Addiction
Recovery" (master's thesis, New York University), 6, https://research
.steinhardt.nyu.edu/scmsAdmin/media/users/_ECEthesisprojects
/Individual_theses/Boyd_Thesis.pdf.

p. 48   *According to the American Heart Association, your brain*: "Spend
Time in Nature to Reduce Stress and Anxiety," American Heart
Association, updated August 1, 2018, https://www.heart.org/en
/healthy-living/healthy-lifestyle/stress-management/spend
-time-in-nature-to-reduce-stress-and-anxiety.

p. 48   *Another study found that a ninety-minute walk in nature*: Rob
Jordan, "Stanford Researchers Find Mental Health Prescription:
Nature," *Stanford News*, June 30, 2015, https://news.stanford.edu
/news/2015/june/hiking-mental-health-063015.html.

p. 48   *While disease prevention is complex, according to*: University of East
Anglia, "It's Official: Spending Time Outside Is Good for You,"
Science Daily, July 6, 2018, www.sciencedaily.com/releases
/2018/07/180706102842.htm.

p. 49   *A study published in the* Journal of Environmental Psychology: Jia
Wei Zhang et al., "An Occasion for Unselfing: Beautiful Nature
Leads to Prosociality," *Journal of Environmental Psychology* 37
(March 2014), https://www.sciencedirect.com/science/article/abs
/pii/S0272494413000893.

p. 49   *A very interesting study showed that even one wilderness expedition*: These details come from Jo Barton et al., "The Wilderness
Expedition: An Effective Life Course Intervention to Improve
Young People's Well-Being and Connectedness to Nature," *Journal
of Experiential Education* 39, no. 1 (January 26, 2016), 59–72,
https://journals.sagepub.com/doi/10.1177/1053825915626933;
and Daniel Bowen, James Neill, and Simon Crisp, "Wilderness
Adventure Therapy Effects on the Mental Health of Youth
Participants," *Evaluation and Program Planning* 58 (October 2016),
https://www.sciencedirect.com/science/article/pii/S01497189153
00094.

Chapter 5: Cut Down on Sugar

p. 53   *The average American consumes seventeen teaspoons (sixty-eight
grams) of sugar*: "Cut Down on Added Sugars," *Dietary Guidelines
for Americans 2015–2020*, March 2016, https://health.gov/sites
/default/files/2019-10/DGA_Cut-Down-On-Added-Sugars.pdf.

p. 55   *an infographic developed by Niraj Naik*: Niraj Naik, "What Happens
One Hour After Drinking a Can of Coke," Renegade Pharmacist,
May 3, 2015, https://therenegadepharmacist.com/what
-happens-one-hour-after-drinking-a-can-of-coke.

p. 58   *In fact, excessive consumption of sugar damages areas of the brain*:
Amy Reichelt, "Why Sugar Is So Much Worse for Teenagers' Brains,"
The Conversation, October 25, 2016, https://theconversation.com
/why-sugar-is-so-much-worse-for-teenagers-brains-67238.

p. 58   *eating too much sugar causes your body to release insulin*: Katherine
Marengo, "Your Anxiety Loves Sugar. Eat These 3 Things Instead,"
Healthline, June 23, 2020, https://www.healthline.com/health
/mental-health/how-sugar-harms-mental-health#highsand-lows.

p. 58   *A 2017 study showed that men who ate sixty-seven*: Anika Knuppel,
"Sugar Intake from Sweet Food and Beverages, Common Mental
Disorder, and Depression: Prospective Findings from the Whitehall
II Study," *Scientific Reports* 7 (July 27, 2017), https://www.nature
.com/articles/s41598-017-05649-7.

p. 58   *However, did you know it also damages your skin, liver*: Locke
Hughes, "How Does Too Much Sugar Affect Your Body?" WebMD,
updated December 17, 2019, https://www.webmd.com/diabetes
/features/how-sugar-affects-your-body.

p. 59   *Overconsumption of sugar causes addiction through its chemical
process*: Nicole Avena, Pedro Rada, and Bartley Hoebel, "Evidence
for Sugar Addiction: Behavioral and Neurochemical Effects of
Intermittent, Excessive Sugar Intake," *Neuroscience & Biobehavioral
Reviews* 32, no. 1 (2008), https://www.ncbi.nlm.nih.gov/pmc/articles
/PMC2235907.

Chapter 6: Manage Your Time

p. 70   *Research shows that students who achieve mostly As*: Amy R.
Wolfson and Mary A. Carskadon, "Understanding Adolescents'
Sleep Patterns and School Performance: A Critical Appraisal,"
Sleep Medicine Reviews 7, no. 6 (December 2003): 491–506,
https://pubmed.ncbi.nlm.nih.gov/15018092.

p. 70   *The University of London found that multitasking*: "To Multitask
or Not to Multitask," University of Southern California, Dornsife
College of Letters, Arts, and Sciences, https://appliedpsychology
degree.usc.edu/blog/to-multitask-or-not-to-multitask.

p. 71   *In a study of nursing students*: Arezoo M. Ghiasvand et al.,
"Relationship between Time Management Skills and Anxiety and
Academic Motivation of Nursing Students in Tehran," *Electronic
Physician* 9, no. 1 (January 25, 2017), https://www.ncbi.nlm.nih.gov
/pmc/articles/PMC5308512.

p. 71   *A study of engineering students at Baylor University*: Walter Bradley
and Steven Bradley, "Increasing Retention by Incorporating
Time Management and Study Skills into a Freshman Engineering

Course," Proceedings of the 2004 American Society for Engineering Education Annual Conference & Exposition, June 20, 2004, https://peer.asee.org/increasing-retention-by-incorporating-time -management-and-study-skills-into-a-freshman-engineering -course-2004.

p. 71   *A study revealed that students who perceived that*: Therese Macan et al., "College Students' Time Management: Correlations with Academic Performance and Stress," *Journal of Educational Psychology* 82, no. 4 (December 1990), https://psycnet.apa.org /buy/1991-13852-001.

Chapter 7: Manage Your Money

p. 79   *In fact, a 2015* Journal of Consumer Affairs *article*: Terri Friedline, "A Developmental Perspective on Children's Economic Agency," *Journal of Consumer Affairs* 49, no. 1 (January 24, 2015), https://onlinelibrary.wiley.com/doi/full/10.1111/joca.12062.

p. 84   *In a study on how income affects the brain*: These details come from Olga Khazan, "How Income Affects the Brain," *Atlantic*, May 15, 2018, https://www.theatlantic.com/health/archive/2018/05/how-in come-affects-the-brain/560318; and Carolyn Gregoire, "How Money Changes the Way You Think and Feel," *Greater Good Magazine*, February 8, 2018, https://greatergood.berkeley.edu/article/item /how_money_changes_the_way_you_think_and_feel.

p. 85   *Having more money increases our subjective well-being*: These details come from Cassie Mogilner, Ashley Whillans, and Michael Norton, "Time, Money, and Subjective Well-Being," in E. Diener, S. Oishi, and L. Tay, eds., *Handbook of Well-Being* (Salt Lake City, UT: DEF Publishers, 2018), https://www.hbs.edu/faculty/Publication%20 Files/Time,%20Money,%20and%20Subjective%20Well-Being _cb363d54-6410-4049-9cf5-9d7b3bc94bcb.pdf; and "How Does Money Impact Well-Being?," University of Minnesota, https://www .takingcharge.csh.umn.edu/how-does-money-impact-wellbeing.

p. 85   *Studies have concluded that financial stress influences our physical health*: Emily Brown Weida, Pam Phojanakong, Falguni Patel, and Mariana Chilton, "Financial Health as a Measurable Social Determinant of Health," *PLOS ONE* 15, no. 5, May 18, 2020, https:// journals.plos.org/plosone/article?id=10.1371/journal.pone.0233359.

Chapter 8: Have Healthy Relationships

p. 92 *In fact, relationships can affect our health just as much as sleep*: "The Health Benefits of Strong Relationships," Harvard Health Publishing, Harvard Medical School, updated August 6, 2019, https://www.health.harvard.edu/newsletter_article/the-health -benefits-of-strong-relationships.

p. 96 *A 2019* Wall Street Journal *article reported that the twenties*: Clare Ansberry, "At What Age Do You Meet Your Best Friend?" *Wall Street Journal,* July 14, 2019, https://www.wsj.com/articles/at-what-age -do-you-meet-your-best-friend-11563109200.

p. 101 *When you fall in love, you turn on the pleasure center of your brain*: Alvin Powell, "When Love and Science Double Date," *Harvard Gazette,* February 13, 2018, https://news.harvard.edu/gazette/story /2018/02/scientists-find-a-few-surprises-in-their-study-of-love.

p. 101 *Studies have shown that the elderly, for example*: These details come from "Friendships: Enrich Your Life and Improve Your Health," Mayo Clinic, August 24, 2019, https://www.mayoclinic.org /healthy-lifestyle/adult-health/in-depth/friendships/art-20044860; and "Science Update: Positive Family Relationships in Adolescence May Reduce Depression Risk During Midlife, NIH-Funded Study Suggests," National Institutes of Health, November 13, 2019, https://www.nichd.nih.gov/newsroom/news/111319-adolescent -family-relationships.

p. 102 *Stress can adversely affect your coronary arteries, gut function*: These details come from "Health Benefits," Harvard Health Publishing; and "Friendships: Enrich Your Life," Mayo Clinic.

p. 102 *One study asked young-adult couples to talk*: Emily Esfahani Smith, "Masters of Love," *Atlantic,* June 12, 2014, https://www.theatlantic .com/health/archive/2014/06/happily-ever-after/372573.

Chapter 9: Be Mindful

p. 111 *According to studies, practicing mindfulness meditation*: These details come from Sabrina Stierwalt, "Mindfulness: The Science Behind the Practice," *Scientific American,* December 17, 2018, https://www.scientificamerican.com/article/mindfulness-the -science-behind-the-practice; and Bruce Lieberman, "Mindfulness

May Have Been Overhyped," *BBC*, May 7, 2018, https://www
.bbc.com/future/article/20180502-does-mindfulness-really-improve
-our-health.

p. 112   *Several studies have found that mindfulness*: These details come
from Miguel Farias and Catherine Wikholm, "Has the Science of
Mindfulness Lost Its Mind?" *BJPsych Bulletin* 40, no. 6 (December
2016), https://www.ncbi.nlm.nih.gov/pmc/articles/PMC5353526;
Stierwalt, "Mindfulness"; and Alvin Powell, "When Science Meets
Mindfulness," *Harvard Gazette*, April 9, 2018, https://news.harvard
.edu/gazette/story/2018/04/harvard-researchers-study-how
-mindfulness-may-change-the-brain-in-depressed-patients.

p. 112   *Studies have proven that mindfulness practice lowers*: Lieberman,
"Mindfulness May."

p. 113   *Mindfulness practice can lead to a healthier diet*: Stierwalt,
"Mindfulness."

p. 113   *Several studies suggest that mindfulness practice*: Daphne Davis and
Jeffrey Hayes, "What Are the Benefits of Mindfulness," *Monitor on
Psychology* 43, no. 7 (July–August 2012), https://www.apa.org/monitor
/2012/07-08/ce-corner.

Chapter 10: Be Grateful

p. 122   *A 2017 study examined the effects of gratitude*: Joshua Brown and
Joel Wong, "How Gratitude Changes You and Your Brain," *Greater
Good Magazine*, June 6, 2017, https://greatergood.berkeley.edu
/article/item/how_gratitude_changes_you_and_your_brain.

p. 122   *Actively practicing gratitude has positive effects*: These details come
from Manju Singh, Waheeda Khan, and Meena Osmany, "Gratitude
and Health Among Young Adults," *Indian Journal of Positive
Psychology* 5, no. 4 (2014), https://www.questia.com/library/journal
/1P3-3591963141/gratitude-and-health-among-young-adults; Kiralee
Schache et al., "Gratitude — More than Just a Platitude? The
Science Behind Gratitude and Health," *British Journal of Health
Psychology* 24 (November 28, 2018), https://onlinelibrary.wiley.com
/doi/abs/10.1111/bjhp.12348; and Claudia Wallis, "The New Science
of Happiness," *Time*, January 17, 2005, labs.psychology.illinois.edu
/~ediener/Documents/Time-Happiness.pdf.

p. 123   *In one study of what's called the "three things exercise"*: Jodi Schulz,

"Gratitude Part 3: Health Benefits," Michigan State University Extension, May 16, 2018, https://www.canr.msu.edu/news/gratitude _part_3_health_benefits.

p. 123 *Related to this is the fact that gratitude makes you more patient*: Schulz, "Gratitude Part 3."

p. 124 *It improves both sleep quality and sleep duration*: Randy Sansone and Lori Sansone, "Gratitude and Well-Being: The Benefits of Appreciation," *Psychiatry MMC* 7, no. 11 (November 2010), https://www.ncbi.nlm.nih.gov/pmc/articles/PMC3010965.

Chapter 11: Hope

p. 131 *Having hope releases the brain's endorphins and enkephalins*: Amanda Enayati, "How Hope Can Help You Heal," *CNN Health*, April 11, 2013, https://www.cnn.com/2013/04/11/health/hope -healing-enayati/index.html.

p. 131 *a study of 231 high school students revealed*: Paul Ratner, "Scientists Find Out How Hope Protects the Brain," *Big Think*, October 20, 2017, https://bigthink.com/hope-optimism/scientists-find-out -how-hope-protects-the-brain.

p. 131 *In one study, five hundred college students participated*: Kirsten Weir, "Mission Impossible," *Monitor on Psychology* 44, no. 9 (October 2013), https://www.apa.org/monitor/2013/10/mission-impossible.

p. 132 *One study on cancer patients measured the amount*: These details come from Devika Duggal, Amanda Sacks-Zimmerman, and Taylor Liberta, "The Impact of Hope and Resilience on Multiple Factors in Neurosurgical Patients," *Cureus* 8, no. 10 (October 2016), https://www.ncbi.nlm.nih.gov/pmc/articles/PMC5120968; and Weir, "Mission Impossible."

p. 132 *Evidence shows that hope is related to better academic*: Duggal, "Impact of Hope."

p. 133 *In studies on patients with or without hope*: Duggal, "Impact of Hope."

About the Author

Kristi Hugstad is on a mission to abolish the stigma of mental illness and suicide, and that starts with teens. Kristi's husband, Bill, completed suicide by running in front of a train after struggling for decades with clinical depression and substance abuse. Their story may have ended differently if they'd known the warning signs and risk factors of depression and suicide, and today Kristi is determined to raise awareness of both, so no one is ever too late to save a loved one.

Kristi Hugstad is the author of *Beneath the Surface: A Teen's Guide to Reaching Out When You or a Friend Is in Crisis*; *What I Wish I'd Known: Finding Your Way through the Tunnel of Grief*; *R U OK?: Teen Depression and Suicide*; and a trilogy of gift books, *Returning to Joy: Inspiration for Grieving the Loss of a Loved One*, *Returning to Joy: Inspiration for Grieving the Loss of Your Dog*, and *Returning to Joy: Inspiration for Grieving the Loss of Your Cat*. She is also a professional speaker, certified grief recovery specialist, grief and loss facilitator for addicts in recovery, and credentialed health educator. Kristi hosts *The Grief Girl* podcast and *The Grief Girl* OC Talk Radio show, and she is a longtime blogger for the *Huffington Post* and *Elephant Journal*. For more information, visit her website, www.thegriefgirl.com.

NEW WORLD LIBRARY is dedicated to publishing books and other media that inspire and challenge us to improve the quality of our lives and the world.

We are a socially and environmentally aware company. We recognize that we have an ethical responsibility to our readers, our authors, our staff members, and our planet.

We serve our readers by creating the finest publications possible on personal growth, creativity, spirituality, wellness, and other areas of emerging importance. We serve our authors by working with them to produce and promote quality books that reach a wide audience. We serve New World Library employees with generous benefits, significant profit sharing, and constant encouragement to pursue their most expansive dreams.

Whenever possible, we print our books with soy-based ink on 100 percent postconsumer-waste recycled paper. We power our offices with solar energy and contribute to nonprofit organizations working to make the world a better place for us all.

Our products are available wherever books are sold. Visit our website to download our catalog, subscribe to our e-newsletter, read our blog, and link to authors' websites, videos, and podcasts.

customerservice@newworldlibrary.com
Phone: 415-884-2100 or 800-972-6657
Orders: Ext. 110 • Catalog requests: Ext. 110
Fax: 415-884-2199

www.newworldlibrary.com